T0207909

THE STORM OF LA NIÑA: A CHRONICLE OF TODAY'S PROFESSIONAL WOMYN

A creative compilation of short stories, rants, letters,
diary entries, speeches, narratives, theoretical analyses,
and poems on the untold ironies of the 50 year old multi-cultured
storm of the professional womyn

LLUVIA DE MILAGROS CARRASCO

Co-publishers:
Angélica H. Salceda, Amber Butts, and Myrna Santiago

authorHOUSE®

AuthorHouse™
1663 Liberty Drive
Bloomington, IN 47403
www.authorhouse.com
Phone: 1 (800) 839-8640

Published by AuthorHouse   02/18/2016

ISBN: 978-1-5049-7068-6 (sc)
ISBN: 978-1-5049-7066-2 (hc)
ISBN: 978-1-5049-7067-9 (e)

Library of Congress Control Number: 2015921471

Print information available on the last page.

This book is printed on acid-free paper.

Dedication:

To The Next Future Powerhouse,
The next beautiful mixed-face soul to be elected,
The next generation of Love to come.

Introduction: Acknowledgements, dedications, and note to the reader

I would be able to write an entirely separate project within itself for all the beautiful souls that have inspired, ignited, and stimulated or simply in silence have contributed in some way to the makings of this publication. Within the small space I have here to give my gratitude and thanks – I would love to acknowledge the following that I have dear in my heart as an extension of my family, blood, and tribe... I want to thank the publication team of editors, marketing strategists, and consultants – Rebecca Duggan, thank you for bringing the logistical support and therefore life of this ever-evolving project and conversation. Thank you, Author House for being the blend of both independent and traditional publishing and making this dream into a reality.

I want to take some time to thank all my sisters from around the world all the way from Utah, Canada, Oregon, Mexico, Indonesia, China, Guam, France, New York, San Francisco, Oakland, Berkeley, San Jose, Washington, Atlanta, Asheville, and more. Thank you sisters who in simple conversation brought many of these themes, topics, and love out of my mind of madness and into therapeutic space – you all healed my words into literature. Thank you Sarah Tepikian, Sarah Fazackerlry, Polly Crookston, Emily Thompson, Carmen Torres, Allie O'neal, Remy Wilder, Megan Hansen, Joy Lingen, Anmol Singh, Lauren Melenbecker, Courtney Jackson, Kiran Gill, Aracely Maravilla, Kelly Foster, Amanda Muña, Alejandra Velasquez, Leah Gonzalez, Elizabeth Palomar, Mayra Hernandez, Karen Gonzalez, Kenna Williams, Scarlett Manzano, Monse Cabrera, Diana Diaz, and my Hermanas Unidas to my fellow Hermandad...

Thank you Mother India, Mother Mexico, Mother Africa, Mother America, and of course my worldly Tribe.

Thank you brothers and humans who have had the patience to co-create with me in this lifetime – Mazin Jamal, Rodney Nickens, Angelica Salceda, Amber Butts, Molly Baker, Zoë Loos, Andee McKenzie, Talya Brott, Rachel Hartley, Eno Emjayy Bong, Lawrence Jones, Wazi Davis, Yanni Lin, and Nathan Sandoval. Now, I would like to send my gratitude to my beloved mentors, co-creators, and ever-evolving lovers in this dream of truth we are fighting into reality. Thank you for joining me in this beautiful revolutionary journey – Myrna Santiago, Mary McCall, David Quijada, Jeannine King, Sweden Larson, Monica Fitzgerald, Cindy Avitia, Vien Troung, Frine Medrano, Conrad Nebecker, Eduardo Salaz, and President of Saint Mary's College of California James Donahue for being an ally and agent of change in higher education. Thank you for the on-going love, support, and space you saw in me that challenged my journey of growth and enlightenment. You all simply gave me the batteries for the flashlight I already had in my hands to give light to the ways of the world.

I want to especially thank my inspiring, hard-working, and resilient family who had the faith in me to not only support but love me unconditionally in my accomplishments as well as my falls whom never saw as failures. Thank you to my dear revolutionary parents Kevin de Leon and Magdalena Carrasco. In addition, my grandparents for making these endless dreams a possibility for generations to come, thank you Abuelito Miguel Carrasco and "Weatha' Maria Carrasco for putting Santiago Papasquiaro and San Nicholas on the map. All the way from San Jose to the rest of the Bay Area and Los Angeles, our name is here in the world of America, forevermore. Thank you to my cousins and Tías for holding dear to my heart the best community of family members and childhood memories I could ever as for – Thank you to the Lomeli's, Montenegro's, Gonzalez's, Bellot's, Diaz's, Jaquez's – Thank you for being my roots.

Last but not least, I would like to especially thank my twin flame and partner in this world who makes this lonely journey not so alone – Thank you Matthew Jacob Moore for being just as crazy as I, and for being the muse to my contributions to this world. I dedicate this project to you all and to the sea of sisters, brothers, and co-creators I have yet to meet but can only hope that these words bring you comfort and discomfort – For I hope, simply, that these words may reach your hearts.

With Universal Love,
Stay Open.
Lluvia de Milagros

Lluvia de Milagros was born in the Bay Area where she spent most of her time growing up, traveling to every nook, city, town, cafe, museum, and bookstore that Northern California could offer. At an early age, Lluvia could be found any given day journaling, reading Calvin and Hobbes, "collaging" her bedroom walls with music posters and CD covers, playing and sadly destroying her grandmothers' wardrobe (pre-thrifting era), dancing, singing, always taking her talent show group performances too seriously, listening to her grandmothers' old Mexican folk tales and ranch songs, cooking potions and new creations that were never edible, painting outside to paste real flowers and leaves to her canvasses, and making up her own games with family and friends.

Growing up always creative and imaginative, she became acutely observant having spent so much time with her at the time, single working mother. Lluvia was a single child living in a mixed generational home of aunts, cousins, her mother and grandparents, where she learned to speak Spanish as her first language and early on became exposed to a community of strong, hard-working, independent and fierce womyn. After having experienced a kidnapping and rape in her early years in High School, Lluvia returned from a Treatment program in Utah to graduate on time at Notre Dame High School in downtown San Jose. Once completing High School, she went off to change numerous majors - Psychology, Sociology, Environmental Studies, Teachers for Tomorrow Program - to finally arrive to Women's and Gender Studies. During her time at Saint Mary's College of California, she completed her minor studies, one summer in Cuernavaca, Mexico then returned to continue teaching throughout the Bay Area in different service programs.

Over four years, Lluvia performed numerous shows with her spoken word pieces, was asked to publish on different media forums and has been interviewed by different radio stations on her creative pieces and poetry work. Lluvia involved herself in numerous student and non-profit organizations in and out of University, was apart of the union efforts her freshman year to unionize Saint Mary's in over 50 years. In addition, joined a Chicana Feminist Writers Collective that was based out of Berkeley and later that year helped coordinate the schools' first Hip-Hop club named "Elements". In her third year, she went off with official credentials to hold communication and observation work for the United Nations in Lima, Peru then later in Paris, France.

By graduation, as a full-time student and now published author, Lluvia is set to pursue her ambitions in the arts – music, creative writing/ screenwriting, scholastics, and politics through what she believes to be an artistic and accessible public platform. Throughout her life, she has witnessed discrimination and trauma for being an ambitious, intrinsic, talented, charismatic, and young woman of color, which has only inspired her even more to resist and challenge the standard of beauty, intelligence, legitimacy, creativity, originality, and power. In all of her publications and creative performances or artistic pieces she has expressed her passion in multiculturalism, transnationalism, queer studies, ethnic studies, youth empowerment, environmental ethics, education equity, civil rights, and diverse inclusivity.

Being the daughter of two elected officials, Lluvia has always believed that she is independent yet parallel to her and her parents' work. However, she resists the idea that she is successful through and under the iconic images of her parents. Lluvia de Milagros, believes overall in the power of the womyn author who has been too many times historically erased -

Dear Reader,

Stay Revolutionary.

Love,

Lluvia de Milagros

_____

"JOURNALS"

Ink is dripping,
Disappearing,
Dissipating
Into my paper where only the marks
Crease my invisible words.

Ink is fading,
But only when I write
It fades away from me...

Search my dear,
For what is inspiration
Search my dear,
For that which cannot,
Does not,
And will not
Fade.

Sometimes poetry
Is the only language that reads me,
Sometimes poetry
Is the only scripture praised to me,

The only rhythm my world dances to

Words you are my drum,
The echo of a heart beat
Seeking to transpire
Into all that I desire

You are the heartbeat
To take my veins
And pulsate
Like the wine
Of the world

Drunk,
Drink off of pure oblivion
Sacred space that has yet to be
Permeated

Oh, Land of Lovelies! What should happen?
When there is no more ink...

And the creased lines
Of a forgotten marking
Simply turns into a licked pen,
A locked pen.

Hoping to still have the blood of my rants,
A series of titles
To writings **yet written...**

--

Rants bleed
My unspoken
And unwritten
Revelations.

--

Section One: Writings of Color

Poetry is when fantasy meets reality.
Too much of either, alone –
Can never exist in each world.

A blend of fantasy and reality
Explores the soul existence,
The soul discovery

Of creative equilibrium.

"Mentally Disturbed, Mujer Soy"

Mentally disturbed, Mujer Soy.
Words already set me up to fail.
Oh, how language and words forevermore,
Will never keep up.

Una mezcla de mundos[1],
Una mezlca de tiempos,
De sangres,
De historias,

Construiendo mi lengua de vivir.

Ahh..
And still,
I am not nearly articulate enough;

--

And my mind races...
Infiltrating the language
My soul already carries
With the whispers that my ancestors speak,
As they swim within my young blood,
My young,
Naive,
19-year-old
American - Mexican
Chicana - Activist
Educated - Latina

---

[1] Translation: "Una Mezcla de mundos, Una mezcla de tiempos, de sangres, de historias, construiendo mi lengua de vivir"
"A mix of worlds, a mix of times, of bloods, of histories, constructing my tongue to live."

And still,
Young,
Naive,
19-year-old blood...

--

Swimming,
Exploring –

The whispers trail upstream

Where my mind soars,

As if this human shell
Can dare to clip my wings?

And there,
My disturbance begins…
The internal battle of what is true
And what is advertised as truth,

That there,
That is my madness.

My wicked Madness,
My womanly Madness,
My beautiful Madness.

Nevertheless,
It is MY madness.

And they say I am
Too Mexican for the Americans,
Too American for the Mexicans.

Too bohemian for the hommies,
Too gangster for the hippies.
Too free-spirited;
Such as the Hummingbird Goddess
Of our Aztec Mothers.

Yet too raw,
Too real,
Too roughened by life
Such as the piercing wisdom,
The warrior spirit
Of our Native American Fathers.

--

Treating knowledge as if I am enmeshed

Or madly obsessed,
Never missing the kernels of truth,

Refusing to lead a misspent youth.

The appetite of curiosity inside,
Hunger, that I refuse to let die.
With sight of the light
Waiting to ignite.

And the hands of the mind,
Never tied.

--

Too politically aware for the youth,
Too grounded for the drugs,
Yet way too high on life & culture to conform,
Or maybe too humanly frightened,

To let the fuck go.

Into this White Wonderland,
Paradox of a Wonderland,
A wonder-hand.

Such as a passing butterfly would be
As she migrates through the summer breeze,
With the rays of the sun,
Shining through the fibers of her wings.

Beaming through the whiskers of her antennas.

Just as she would be,
When the summer warmth
Hits
It's first Winter Flake.

Gazing over the flawless,
Powdered blanket of a wonderland.

And oh, what a wonder it is…
What a wonder it truly is…

--

Pero así camino en mi Tierra[2],
Cada paso lo lleno,
De las melodías de mi oscuridad
Del espiritú de mis lagrimas,

---

[2] Translation: "Pero así camino en mi Tierra, cada paso lo lleno, de las melodías
de mi oscuridad, del espiritú de mis lagrimas, con colores de fé, con colores
de ser humano, asi camino en mi Tierra…"
"But that is how I walk on my Land, with each step I fill with the melodies of
my darkness, with the spirit of my tears and sorrows, with the colors of faith,
the colors of being human, this is how I walk on my Land."

Con colores de fé,
Con colores de ser humano
Asi camino en mi Tierra...

--

The unorthodox path that she migrates through
Is simply her bittersweet burden
?

--

Again, this is my Madness.
My wicked Madness.
But Blessed Madness,
And oh
So beautiful of a Madness.

Hmmm... mentally disturbed;
Is simply to be Educated.
As A minority of The minority.

Womanly Disturbed;
Is simply to be Revolutionary
Again, as
A minority of The Minority.

To struggle with your
Political depression,

Academic racism,

Cultural dichotomy.

And STILL - find presence in the present.

For this wonderland of a land,
Is seasonal.

And carved with each colorful footprint,
With each lining of your toe,
As it marks your skin's signature -

Leading & Leaving.
Like the artist that you are.
Painting & Printing.

I continue to draw on this wonderland,
Of a Wonderful Land.

And in my hand,
My Brush.
For my Paper,
My World.
And my paint,
My Love.

Disturbed with a beautifully tortured,
Humanistic soul;

I will continue to paint,
I will continue to migrate,
I will continue to fuel the ember in me.

Mentally Disturbed,
Me-disturbed,
Mujer Soy.

And that is the butterfly
Soaring in me.

"Awaiting to Awake"

Cansada morenita[3],
Cansada de lo que soy

Estrella morenita
Mi Linda aqui estoy

Abremé la ventana
Respira de ser Chicana

Saludos al universo
Y todo que es hermoso

Si mi cansada morenita,
Brilla de sueños latente
latente pero todavia soñando

Y desapareciendo sin ser desaparecida
Estrella morenita,
Dejas de existir

You cease to exist!

Cansada morenita,

---

[3] "Cansada morenita, Cansada de lo que soy, Estrella morenita, Mi Linda aqui estoy, Abremé la ventana, Respira ser de Chicana, Saludos al universo, Y todo que es hermoso, Si mi cansada morenita, Brilla de sueños latent, latente pero todavia soñando, Y desapareciendo sin ser desaparecida, Estrella morenita, Dejas de existir"

"Tired brown girl, tired of what I am, my shining brown star, my love I am here. Open me the window, breathe in the air of a Chicana life, greet the Universe, and all that is beautiful. Yes, my tired brown girl, shine of dormant dreams, dormant and still dreaming, you are disappearing but never missing. My shining brown star, you cease to exist."

Cansada de lo que soy

Estrella morenita,
Mi amor aqui estoy

Aqui estoy

Double-tongued Malinche[4]

I, too

Speak the language of two

---

[4]   Malinche refers to a Mexican local term that is considered to be an insult to women, such as calling upon a woman as a traitor or a manipulative snake. The term originated as the mistress of Cortés who later translated as the only indigenous princess that could speak more than one language. However, it is rarely seen that Malinche and her intelligence was used against her naivety for not being able to predict an era of conquest that was soon after unfolded through the bridge of her translations. Many students and political organizers that attempt to reclaim the origins and impact of the word Malinche seek in modern day to reclaim and resist the negative connotation of the words' evolving definition.

"Freedom falling into"

There she flies in a speck

A speck that is
Spectacular

Every person ever lived,
Ever died,
Runs

In the meadows
That society plants

Planting,
Growing,
& Nourishing

For good or bad – she is planted

FOR the Good,
FOR the Bad

Planted underground, a hidden gem...

She waits for the next raining season
Where the next water drops

To where the next leaf falls
And embarks...

Look at her in her natural state,
Just look at her

Uncovered.
Bare.

With skin
As light
Or as dark
As it should.

The only difference between her and that neighbor
Are our ancestors' geographic planes

Planes that could not yet "fly" to another state
Generations that have been blessed with more sun,

For it was hot,
So hot...

Hot land that birthed
The fire of a heavy heart,
A young heart,
A heart exploring the planes
Of a world yet known,

Yet touched,

Yet discovered.

And thus,
Skin is toasted,

With the burning heat of a (his)tory –
And therefore, (she)story
Rather; (our)story.

Yes, generations that received more sun
Than that neighbor
Whomever...

Because it was hot
So, very, hot.

Hot as the fire that burns her soul.
Became the same heat

That sings a nueva cancion

Hot as the nature of a Nopal...
Makings of melatonin
And majestic Madonnas

The land loves
The Soft-spoken sanctuary
Of a shining Sapphire

...

At the end of the day
We share the same beat
Singing the melodies of a common truth
& With the same background noise,
With the same human cravings

...

Desires,
Disturbances,
Pleasures with pain...
All while we seek to survive.
Surviving for curiosity
Curiosity of the future alive

What it may or may not pertain
We believe we have the control

Control to ourselves,
& Other wounds

Control to dictate this map,
A blueprint of an infrastructure
That has yet to rise

--

Human nature,
Complicated
Unknown,
And faded.

Yet familiar,
Wise - in every part of its everlasting fade

--

As it slips through our finger tips,
It drips onto a new hand

And there it recycles and re-energizes,

Both living and fading
In the nature of pure evolution.

Just like evolution,
She drops her thoughts,
At times giving in…

Naturally
To religion,
School,
And even a boyfriend,
A girlfriend - replaced

Yet forgets she is as free
Always as free
And as unpredictable
As the leaf she is

The Madonna she is
The sapphire she is
Falling,
Illuminating
& Shining

Always in a different place

To a different place
From a different place

Falling,
Illuminating,
Shining

Yes, falling like the wild leaf
…But not always down,

For she is

Freedom
Falling
Into.

Falling into place,
As the Madonna
And as the Sapphire.

Letters to a sister

My dear sister,

I do not know of what you are going through nor do I need to know the details to (not inform you of matters you, yourself already possess and know in the depths of your being) but simply to REMIND you (again, of what you already know, but what we can tend to forget from time to time) and that is the amazing power we hold as humans - the power that creates the most beautiful, soulful works of ourselves in this world, and that is the power to possess our true happiness. Look at who you are today Angelica***, for better or for worse, your trials & tribulations have occurred for a reason. And those troubles will continue to seep into the most unexpected times in our lives, never ending - we must accept, that they are in fact - never ending. But they shouldn't be shamed, they shouldn't be ignored, they shouldn't be denied. For it is, what I believe, the universe's reminder - of our own power. Our own abilities, our own control (of the very little we can in fact, control).

As a woman, our thirst will never perish. Will never be satisfied. Will never be fully understood by those who do not quench what we as women, starve for. That is the price we pay, as this unique species that we are, that we are not only distinguished as HUMANS from the rest of the animal kingdom – our queendom – but even more, Woman, Woman of Human. Woman of Human, who will understand WHEN and where to be satisfied - but that is not HIS power that is OURS. That is OUR power, OUR control, and OUR force in which we birth into love.

Womyn, we are revolutionary in pure physical, spiritual, psychological and biological structure. We are the spirit that travels trough the vessels of life and the veins of the earths' heartbeat, because we are the hands of women and therefore the fingerprints of Humanity.

You ARE Life.
NEVER forget it.
This is the Malinche seed.
Nostalgia be my poison

--

Sun-kissed speckled sonrisas,
Smile the sunrise of your own salvation

Dearest One,

As women of color, we are performers – so, as a modern woman of color – I am a professional performer. So why not make money off of it?

--

Intersecionality[5] at its finest.

And here in my notes, even as I type away into 2016, I must "add" such an "in-autocorrected" word… Oh the irony continues.

--

Stop comparing apples to oranges when speaking about oppression,

There is no room for judgment for you are the present looking at a moment that happened in the past,

THAT moment which was accumulated by a universe of micro beings of life coming together at its natural equation for that one moment that became infinite in its very limited space in time.

That one moment that because the pebbles in which you step to the left, and at times to the right, in order to leap on that mountain of a rock to make your world, your island that blocked the flow of the river… So that you can make that island yours and come on to the other side of the riverbed.

---

[5]   intersectionalitySyllabification: in·ter·sec·tion·al·i·ty
Pronunciation: /ˌin(t)ərsekSHəˈnalədē/
Definition of *intersectionality* in English: **Noun : The interconnected nature of social categorizations such as race, class, and gender as they apply to a given individual or group, regarded as creating overlapping and interdependent systems of discrimination or disadvantage:*through an awareness of intersectionality, we can better acknowledge and ground the differences among us' (Oxford Dictionary)*

Moments that you judge, in the name of "understanding" and "enlightenment" – this judgment of apples to oranges, of two worlds stretched apart from one another – two different contexts, two different entities divided always by some kind of wall.

These moments here that we judge such as judging a caterpillar and its cocoon for being in its stage only to shed like a snake into the skin of a butterfly…

Judging the caterpillar for not being a butterfly, and then judging the butterfly for not having the safety in youth such as the caterpillar. Then return to judging the caterpillar for not having the wings to fly only to judge the butterfly yet again, for the colorful patterns created on its very wings.

We have been trained to never learn how to unlearn. Trained to religiously believe to judge these moments as if we can blame the winter for being cold, and the summer for not being winter, or Fall not being Spring…

Why judge the seasons of life, or the metamorphous in the law of nature for being in its natural course?

Do not be ashamed for being the butterfly that no longer has the shielded naivety of being a caterpillar cocooned…No.

Do not torment yourself into a hell on this Earth for not being "THE" shinning sun kissed summer sunsets –for you rather live life blanketed by a foggy breeze of a dreamy day.

No, my dear –

Do not judge yourself for the seasons of growth.

Do not compare apples to oranges, or chiles to bottled n' capped Tapatio hot sauces.

Do not judge the past for its present and now the present, preset for the future, captivated only by the past, No…

Simply perform.

For you are the Director, the actor, and the audience of your own Play.

For you to play in, and the world to have the privilege in attending such a grand show.

Forever yours,
Lluvia de Milagros

[Breed]

I am my own breed,
A suffocating minority
See, I'm am a competitor
So I become your majestic

Predator

It's this same need
That births the same

Seed

Body be an everlasting shell
I ache for a story to tell

Wisdom hits like a rolling wave
Fearless from every lil' goddamn thang

Enslaved to what you once knew
To every little thing you must undo

I am my own breed
I am my own breed

A creation of
My own entity

"Cenote"

Al cenote me voy,
Al cenote me quedo[6].

Through time,
You drop,
And build upon me.

Redefining my sculpture
Bringing the light,
Into my Allegory cave.

Such as seeing the light
For the first time in a dark room
The power of a switch
Sends a shock through the body

Consumed of light
And in pure discomfort

Startled by brightness
For it becomes a reminder

---

[6]   Cenote: Mexico: A natural deposit of spring water
       "Al cenote me voy, al cenote me quedo"
       "To the deposit of spring water, I go. In the deposit of spring water, I stay.

Of a new sight
My lonely cave,
All I have known to be…

It is home,
The roots,
The leaves,

The depth of its waters…
Into the unknown

Al cenote me voy[7],
En el cenote me encuentro.

---

[7]   "Al cenote me voy, En el cenote me encuentro."
"To the deposit of spring water, I go. In the deposit of spring water, I find myself."

Let the roots

Of life

Seep down

Let me quench

Off of

Your story

"Mexicana: Americana"

My mother became a woman
When she had me

Yes, my mother became a woman,
Only with thee

'I can sense my children'
She will say

'Only to be a woman
Is when I lay'

Look at me be a woman
To this day

In the Mexican eye,
Is to be a slave.

Yes I am woman

Woes with man
Woman.

Woes with man,

Woe in a man,

Woe with your man,

Is Woman

?

Internal Dialogue of a National Actress:

"Mexicana, La Raza Cósmica"

I knew I was the only in the room

(State it as if it were this depressing realization, & then... No...)

I knew I was the only in the room

(State again but as if it were this beautiful realization)

I still should have worn the suit, why did I wear the dress...

The National actress,
Slayin sleek city lights and sights,

Polychild,
The two-edged sword
Of an empress.

I've gotta say...
So long as you have good work ethic...

You will learn
You will rise
And you will lead

This reality,
Merely a canvass to paint our future
And the future,
A canvass redrafting,
And everlasting.

"It's nothing but an illusion"
Says the Communication Director.

"Colonia Libertad"

I'm at the border of San Diego and Tijuana,
Passing Colonia Libertad…

And here in this moment,
A simple wall
Becomes a border.

As I turn my American disposition off,
And change my vestido[8] –

I rap a rebozo[9] over my head,
And I psychologically
Assimilate
Between apples and oranges –
Dried chiles and bottles of Tapatio[10]
All for the "Authentic"
Mexican taco.

I am from both
Aqui y (ni) de allá[11],

And I pass all the señores[12]
Selling Chiclets
On the entrance-exit
Of Colonia Libertad –

---

[8]   Vestido: Dress

[9]   Rebozo: Traditional shawl wrapped around shoulder or head, locally-based and different in tradition depending on where you are, how you wrap, and where you go dressed in the garment.

[10]   Tapatio: Hot sauce bottled and distributed throughout the Untied States

[11]   "Aqui y (ni) de allá" Translation: "Here and (neither) from there"

[12]   Señores: Typically refers to elder men, gentlemen.

Colonia Libertad,
"Neighborhood Freedom"

Is the last neighborhood
Before the gates
Of America

As America
Will open-close.

"Blood, Unnamed."

> **Be loved, Beloved**
> **Your Love is too thick**
> **Be loved, my Beloved**
> **Your love makes me sick...**

I learned from the seas of the Internet, the aesthetics of my ancestry. A medium reflected through the pixelated computer screen becomes my time travel machine. I live through the injustices of my 'ancestors' around this "modern" world, the narrative of hybridity, the unspoken language of a universal vessel with the mask of a mixed face. The stories of untouched - 'untouched' & yet, Literally - forgotten names, that I can feel vibrate & pulsate in my soul, through the shining rays of a musky moonlight as if the dark & magical night is trying to dull... of bodies I could never meet in this life, shells of bodies this realm pushed from human to hermit, never traveled in this time, this life - Nightly, through the conglomerate of teeny-tiny sparks seen to us as stars,

NIGHTLY,

They speak to my veins,

Of bitter-sweet-tastin' of copper -roasted -creamy -coldN'warm-
smoky-deserted- dried –chiles - drowningN'waters- of an everlasting
storm-tongue-tied-freely, enslaved to the will of liberation-Godly-
Dirt Brown, Dirt Poor, Dirt Black but never Dirty, never dirt- Godly
& impure of this lifes' standards of 'purity'-withered-traveled-
aged beyond years-like the aromas of a red-marooned - waitin'
to be drank-drunkened wine- aged, creased like the wrinkles
formed prematurely grasping for the air of these darkened pupils-
embracing and prickled-by the thorns of a gently picked rose-
rather, a gently picked fruit of labor- just to be tossed vigorously
onto the aggressions of a splinter-infected burnt wooden crate- the
redness of an aged rose, handled with love and care and solitude,
only to be fed to the mouth of an entire planct, with the stomach
of three families- red-prickled-aged-sunburnt rose that is shaved

of its traces and thorns is now beautifully placed in the stillness of an imported hand crafted ceramic vase, bought in downtown & made by the very wrinkled-prickled-aged-wounded-infested-soil, under the tips of a finger nail, so thick, its becomes its own nail-such as the stillness of a photograph, framed in fancies for the world to admire & decorate-aged, red, roasted, creamy-warm-bittersweetTastin' of copper-smoky-chile-nagchampa-suffocating and dried and still, yet drowning - beautiful red blood... Yes.

They speak to my veins,
Of Blood that is unnamed.

#2

"Titles to writings yet written"

"Whatever sun set, or sun rise, ya gotta let that sun shine"

"I like the spark that I see in the eyes of your ambitions"

"I am what I am not, & I am not what I am, an illogical logic to follow."

"The language of a look, Becomes the science of your stare"

"She's a model, molded into perfection, direction, and intention"

"Body be a shell, Give me a story to tell"

"I am my own breed, and therefore a minority"

"I am but a competitor, predator"

"Wisdom hits like a rolling wave, leaving you out of breathe from everything you once knew to everything you must undo"

"The same need births the same breed"

"Walking in the background, I am a fly on the wall, and I can listen through my illiterate ears you think are deaf"

"So be loved, Beloved. You do not have to be 'Forever 21'"

"I like the spark I see in the eyes of your ambitions"

"POETRY OUTLINE: Form, Content, Delivery, Context"

"I discovered the world through my book, felt the vibrations of this land with my foot, rumbled through the musky night, with this car, only to get lost in a bar."

"In my cloud of molecules, drifting with the wind, and making love to the storm, so that when the skies clear, we glisten with the worlds' might, and your light, your time, your right, its your shine, yes, your right, and alright, and oh, so, very, might."

"Addicted to ambition"
"Sun, a song sang to a son"
"Nothing is religion and religion becomes nothing. However, to reach God, one must be religious.

"2k away from sec. 8"

"Pulgrosa"

"Analco: AL otro lado del rio"

"The generation of generics"

"Applause"

"Habited listening can never hear"

"Blue Boy, Pinkie – Niño Azul, Rosita"

"Ego so high, no lie."

"Nostalgia is my drug."

"Los de allá": A love story of the legend of 'La Monja de Catedral'"

When there is a lack of culture, you gravitate desperately
and exaggerate the entire relationship with culture as a way
to stay connected, speaking the language of many.

Section Two: Writings of Revelation

"4AM"

A mourning morning, I moan.

Always, in the age of "becoming"...

Always at four in the morning.

"Morning Risers"

I will let you know,
That I am legally illegal
& Illegally leading life

Love me lover,
Lay me life a lovely light
Pounding you are in my hands,
Profoundly, Pounding, Power
You are in my hands

Hard hands,
Hungry Hands,
& Healing Hands

Fly for fiery,
Fighting,
& Frightening,
Forevermore,
Fiery friends

Fly for me,
Freedom,
Fly into me,
Fly with me.

I will let you know,
My child,
My earthling

How painful, purification, pleases…
Precious, painful, purification
Praise the pink,
Pedals that prance
Playfully,
Purifying.

"..."

Oh shit -
what's that right there?
That right there on the wall
right there,
no look up,
and have a good stare

Cus what you see, don't fool the eye,
And what you see is my ego right

And so you Watch
-watch that shit rain,
Cus wait
Ohh shit,
that's my name

And no
I don't mean no symbolism
Cus That queen b

goddess of a ma,
you see

That queen-a-ling
titled me as rain fall,
So you heard that?

(Yepp, Got it doll)

So y'all listen
To My whispered breeze of nostalgia,

Road-trippin up & down Georgia

Birthing the beat of my mami-ahhh

And that
Which Diagnosed my poetic bound insomnia,

But Medicated me with that sun-kissed
California,

Dedicated To my early-morn boss-I-ness-nia,

Yah

Cus I hold on to my sun-kissed passion
As I breathe in y'all's reaction
To the fiery inspiration,
I draft to redraft
my own damn equation
To fuck off that fucking discrimination

I Become eternity,
And the infinity
That I be

So what? we a bit a nerdy,
But you know why?
Cus we people worthy

And We breathe in desire
Just to let out that smoky fire
As we continue to aspire
And re-inspire
So don't get it twisted sire
That this right here
Lluvia de milagros

Uhh ...
she's ya empire

Wah!

Yeah, That's the name
Rainfall of miracles
I ain't playin no games

Too busy Bustlin, huslin
So when ya check my schedule
Im booked in them books

Why?

Cus we breakin the news,
We aint "makin" the news,

Too involved
Just to freely Evolve

Yes.
we breakn' news not makin news

So that Power to the people,

Can overdo them rules
Overdo them rules!

Rewrite them schools
And create powerpeople tools

Yepp..

See That's the motto,
That's the prayer,
That's the chant that y'all can't hear

Nope

Cus you fail to see

What?

That real power ain't in the dough,
Real Power - ha
It's in ya roll,
And In ya
princess priceless stroll,
And In the way that you hold

-hold,

holdin what's been on ya mind,
And On ya grind,
Fuck that - that brings you to cry
That keeps ya blind
Fuck that - on what money can
O' cannot buy
No

No
Then where?

Real power is where you decide to fly.

Right
Where you can fly
Yepp

Where you can fly

Where you can fly

Like birds flying high
You know how I feel
Birds flying high
You know how I feel

(Sing)
And im feeling good

That's right,
only on where you can fly

Right

Cus we makin it,
Just to break it
And we make it -

make it
makin it
make it rain

Make it rain,
With no shame
Rain to the sane,

And the insane
Always stayin in their lane,

Yepp
Cus when I rain,
I waterfall
that 408

~

& I Rain the truths of my optimism
And my pessimism

fuck all that bullshit criticism

But mostly,
I rain the truths of my own organism
My altruism,
Terrorism
My exorcism

Of my life in a prism,

Right

my life in a prism

Yepp

My life in a prism
And the light
Be the only truths I reveal
Ain't nothing
but my skepticism.

~

Word.

"TIME"

Time, you drip on me

Build upon me

Redefine me

Unwind me

Puncture me

Carve into me

Such as the forming of a cave,

I am a sculpture yet to be engraved.

My dear sister,
Brother,
Fellow humanhood,

I do not know of what you are –I can never feel that exact
pain in which you are withstanding in the depths of your
being – but you are not alone for the humanistic capability
of soulful pain and feeling, brings us into one.

The power we hold as humans is the very power to create the most
beautiful, soulful works of ourselves in this world, forgiveness in
its pursuit – the same power that allows will to flourish, that allows
dreams to become its own God particle and transform into the
magical, biological, psychological and physical forms of a new reality.

The very power that allows us to love a soul to the very power that
brings a simple act of kindness to a cold woman sitting against
the curb of your bus stop – the very power that inspires, to the
very power that can bring peace of mind to a heart at war. Oh, my
double-tongued Malinche, nunca seras "mala" en tu Malinche – I
also speak the language of two. Two, three, shit, even four.

Look at who you are today, slumber into a dream with eyes
wide open, for it is four A.M. For better or worse, history
reminds us to not let it define us. Our texts indoctrinated in
and out of a piece of literature, reminds us, that our stories
were edited – published by the lips of a snow-flaked mouth.

Edited out, one can interpret that as suffocating and chained – I see it as the most beautiful flickering fire of strength that seasons from embers to smoke into a never-ending blanket of flames. It is the same power we hold as humans, that loves, and that hates… That pushes, and pulls. That suffocates, and that creates. Trials and tribulations will continue to seep into the most unexpected times in our lives, never-ending, we must accept that they are in fact, never ending.

Yet, they shouldn't be shamed, they shouldn't be ignored, they shouldn't be denied. For it is, what I believe the Universe's reminder of our own power to choose and not choose, and therefore to be of the chosen. Our own abilities, our own control, of the very little we can in fact, control.

Whatever happened to Humanity?

When Man's gentle touch,
Would spark the crawling-tingling sensation of a kiss.
As it would be,
Should be,
The permission already given
By my lip's caressing embrace.

And Man,
Woman,
Could be entrusted
With one simple stare.

For you knew the language
In which my kisses would breathe,
And even if you did not know,
Such womanly ways,
Or womanly language...

I, HUMAN,
Spoke the same.

Ahh,
But it was your dominance,
That wouldn't listen.

Whatever happened to humanity?
When it was in fact,
The melody of my voice,
That sang words you respected.

And No meant No,
But Yes,
Meant mmm yes, yes, yes.

Because it was the word,
That you respected,
That would transmit a heart's desire.

And my mouth,
Became more than a physical vessel
Of instant pleasure...

"Taming" the selfish needs
Of your primitive human nature
Taming, we always tamin'...

Deprived,
Untamed,
& Wild

You feast to surpass satisfaction.

My mouth instead,
Spoke the art of my soul's language.
And voice,
Was heard.

Because it was my existence,
You listened for.

--

Since the waves of my curving body,
Created a silhouette of ever-lasting mystery.

In which you awed for,

Hunted for,

Praised for,

Humbled for,

Explored for,

Patiently waited for my blessing.

--

Whatever happened to humanity?

When as a human race,
We shared the same land,
The same air,
The same hand,

The same world.

You & I,
Shared the same bed.

When as a human race,
To lay with one,
Was only to confirm a common truth

Oh you see,
For when she opens herself
It is as if Spring
Turns to blossom its first flower,
And with your rain
To bring the first shower.

For just as any other force in the Universe
-This shared world did not birth
From only its waters.

Rather,
The love that was made
When the raindrop reached the land's seed,
And quenched such a parched thirst.
And Equilibrium is reached.

Ahh,
But again,
It was your dominance
That did not listen.

--

The Human,
Disillusioned.
By one's own self-perpetuating lies.

The Human,
Therefore governed,

By one's very own despise.

The Human,
Thus cultivated,
By one's very own silent cries.

--

What happened to Humanity?

When in being humanistically
Human,
Our tolerance becomes perfectly
Imperfect,

When living by our vile
Virtue,
We become legally
Illegal.

Whatever happened to humanity?
When Man's gentle touch,

Would spark the crawling-tingling
Sensation of a kiss...

As it would be,
Should be.

A Declaration of Sentiments,

A Constitution of Spirits.

"The Devil's Backbone"

Churches cherish and perish,

In the same year,

Institutionally invincible,

Religiously invisible.

"The Beast, La Bestia, Medea[13]"

Lluvia de Milagros & Sarah Tepikian

Dear white van with its crooked and broken door,
On a 35 degree drugged haze of a morning-night,
Dear vehicle without a license plate,
Stationed in front of a motel,
Taken to a Taco Bell...
I dedicate this to you.

You came, you saw,
you think you conquered me.
I made you cum,
I let you see,
That you could Neva
Strip me.

Penetrated by your own truth,
Naivety,
Shielded my youth.

Split these legs
To reveal your own Pandora

Oh honey, how you reek
Of a diseased Aurora

You came and thought you could conquer
With these memories that never blur,

---

[13] Medea: N*oun* Me·dea \mə-'dē-ə\
     Definition of MEDEA
     : an enchantress noted in Greek mythology for helping Jason gain the Golden
     Fleece and for repeatedly resorting to murder to gain her ends. Origin
     of MEDEA
     Latin, from Greek *Mēdeia*. First Known Use: 14th century

But I made you come,
The power of this sanctum,
Just to let you see,
That you could NEVER

Conquer ME.

So, watch me
Wet with wisdom

While your hearts'
A homeless bum

This clit aint cliché

Your poor blind eyes,
Only see grey

Hey! Hay! Hey!
Well, well, you don't say!

Don't you know?
I've always been okay

Hey! Hay! Hey!
Well, well, you don't say!

Yeah, you came,
You saw,
You thought you conquered

But I made you come,
I made you see,
That you could Neva
Handle me.

No, you could Neva
Take on me
Your vain,
I let bleed.

Vampire sick-suck that shit deep.

I've let you to dry,
And I'll leave you to cry –
Because I am way too high,
I've been flying
In this sparklin' sky

Yes,
I've left you to dry –
I've left,

Goodbye.

Dear Higher Education,

What makes you so high? Are you reaching a form of enlightenment that I cannot reach without your guidance? What are all these fancy words that you believe you have created, with recycled thoughts passed through the wisdom of human life – that now, you have accumulated into 'theory' – simply because you have these three letters by your name – "Ph.D."?

There is a lack of both cultural acceptance and academic validation that is institutionally perpetuated. In turn, we produce the lack of transition from theory to contemporary reality. We challenge so much these damaging social constructs that we are set to be apart of and obsessively study in a liberal arts education. Yet, rarely do we see in that obsession, how much we continue the existence of these properties – and dare I say, turn them more into a physical, academic, and philosophical reality than they need to be. No, I am not denying the role and at times damage in which they have historically created for the world. I simply challenge the ways in which we deliver these crucial messages and facilitate such pivotal conversations for a future that is to be changed. In the constant aim of killing such entities that ought to not continuing living – we bring to life daily, that which we are trying to kill.

Institutionally, there is a systematic illusion created for the next generation evolving, as we focus more and more on defining "identity" on how many social constructs we can put next to a name. It becomes the same obsession that romanticizes oppressed narratives into fashionable trends and hot topic social issues on a never-ending social media feed. As we "clock in" and "clock out" we detach ourselves in theory. In the name of "connecting" and befriending a thousand stranger "friends", we have perpetuated a generation of aliases and profile icons. Such as a new profile picture that has been perfectly cropped, filtered, and edited – we create a new and improved version of ourselves that we can only birth into existence on a pixelated screen.

"I am a pansexual, unicorn, African-Mexican, American, scientist, HR business partner, investor, 23 year old, second generation, baseball player, cis-identified-feline-frog" (etc.)

We see these elements, not as parts, which I personally embrace and find to be a healthy understanding of self – rather, we see these socially instituted and contextually imposed attributions as definers, markers, and precursors to the standard of life we expect ourselves to fulfill.

Therefore, in many ways, we begin to track ourselves into a socially constructed predetermined destiny of opportunities and realities.

To even know the traces of hidden history, one must major in Chicano/Latino/African/Ethnic studies. To attain pedagogy and literal academic validation, one must have the privilege to reach such a level of scholarly prestige.

Oh, the irony! To be a woman of color, and only know of what I am once I have gone through a formula of steps – tirelessly attain not one, but many internships and volunteer in various fields or experiences. Maintain a stellar GPA – since you will learn very early on, that it is a number that will define your value, and therefore your worth. Become an applicant then be accepted, for it is a resume that will define the blueprint of your skillset and therefore capabilities. Sacrifice any and all-financial means, for the degree will be the key of a new world. It is the irony, that to follow such coded formulas, you will be an outlier of the very community in which you will have the choice to study. Only to arrive to the day in which one receives a list to check off yet again, the option between Psychology or Ethnic Studies. To have such limited power in the "choice" of a track, a track between two different worlds – the Sciences or decoding hidden histories. We self perpetuate the very mess we are trying to unlearn, in the ironic hope, that we are liberating ourselves from systematic and academic oppressions.

Instead, why are you not teaching my generation that these entities are part of an overall identity that is of one – and more? Such as ornaments that decorate a charming, shining, Christmas tree or such as a prism that depending on the ways in which you rotate – will let a light shine through and give off a different color...

Dear University,

What is this oversaturated word in which you call "diversity"? Diverse bodies based on skin tones are simply diverse demographics in which you can statistically accumulate, quantify, and therefore display to the world like a curated gallery of foreign objects for an anthropological final project. That in which you promote as "diverse"... Do you cultivate a diversified mentality, or have you simply perpetuated stagnancy in the name of a degree? A degree that is as thin as paper, yet as valuable, as life changing, as the life you will live – 2k away from sec.8.

Dear Millennial,

In the name of "activism", "social justice", "justice", and "service" – how has the time you spent listening to lectures develop your adequacy in connecting to that which you serve? What has become of you, to be driven by the rush of "feeling good" and clocking in your social justice volunteers hours on a clipboard? Rather, become soulfully apart of the integrity behind the mission itself. A mission, simply words put into theory, and theory published throughout a course curriculum – to what point has your morality bridged theory into praxis?

There is more of a disservice done to the very communities in which are "served" when the privileged academic lens shields your ethnocentricity. More so, the physiological and psychological implications and harm done to the overall development of one's self-identity is even more terrifying to witness unravel…

Be the agent of change that is both a product of what you are produced of and what you, yourself will produce. Do not romanticize and fashionably trend social justice issues, for that is an injustice within itself. There is nothing romantic about poverty.

As a result, we are truly a divided nation, polarized groups of people, allies, and issues on a spectrum of prioritizing oppression and having political fits online – yet, never truly using the sea of technology as a tool box of intellectual property.

Dearest Higher Education in which I believe, full heartedly is needed in this world…

Dearest University,

Dearest Millennial,

Dearest brother,

Sister,

Fellow human,

Let us not obsess over race, ethnicity, sexuality, age, status, and gender as a definer of whom we are – they are our ornaments if we chose to let them be, but they are not definers of our capabilities.

So why do we perpetuate this mentality that gives constant validity to a social construct as a literal definer? It is the irony that, ironically, we allow to set us apart when it should be that irony that we laugh at and thank for bringing us together.

I know what you are thinking, well who am I then?

And I will tell you…

I am a sister, I am a partner, a scholar, a thinker, an observer, an
outgoing introvert, a daughter born in April, a granddaughter
holding the heart of a warm house of Abuelitos, Tías, primos,
and crispy lightly burnt tortillas always on the comal.

I am a dancer – only when the summer season brings its blanket
of warmth and sun-kissed memories that have yet to be made,
I am a singer – but mostly in the shower, a writer – when a
cloudy day brings to my nostrils the rains' musk, I am an artist,
a soul in seasons, a co-created game-changer, and this body
of a shell happens to be the car that drives me in this life.

I am a co-creator* with an entrepreneurial spirit addicted to ambitions
of making an imprint on this world, a hybrid goddess of what my
parents are and aren't – of what my ancestry never saw to what
my cosmic spirits were never able to historically be honored for,
I am that and more because I am simply an earthling vessel…

I am the bittersweet product of a series of copy-pasted stories,
edited and newly formed words autocorrected, messages lost in
translation, with folk wisdom of oral stories passed down and
forgotten at the day of her funeral, all in the mouth of a white
pink lipped publicist… A rhetoric of a language disappeared
and the narrative that founded, that molded white America
yet was never embraced by its very tribe of authors.

I am a name stored in commodities with a bar code imprinted – yet,
at what point will this bar code be seen as simply a tattoo reminding
the world of such a point in history – permanent on my skin, sure…

But reduced in only a materialistic and physical form.

Permanent on my skin,

But never on my soul.

With unconditional

And universal love,

Lluvia de Milagros

"Passerby"

May this be as poetic as you see,
May this be what you read,
What isn't already put in

Playing the game,
Formulating prophecies

Never as real as it should be
And we only come out
When we choose to

Because greatness
Is born through time
While whispered wisdom
Becomes its creator

Let it flourish when it should,
Let it all be in its own time
Let it all be sacred
And wonderful
As it should

For it is all already within its course

Wisdom,
Becomes the central parent
to all that is great

The most heart wrenching
Burden to live by.

I saw myself in her cry,

A dear passerby.

Reflections of the Alter Ego
Reflections of the Social Mask
Reflections dedicated to Mother Mexico, Father America.
Reflections of the deceased, who cease to exist.

The bittersweet danger with alter egos is that you can run the risk of creating an identity that becomes a costume, similarly to Native American headdresses used at music festivals and Indian bindis used as a fashion statement. Identity is never a costume but rather a reality. When you detach yourself from the alter ego, you detach from all that encompasses the validity of an identity, because you have reduced this representation of a world of histories, stories, and universes – to a Halloween costume.

On the contrary, the beauty of a culture, the sweet balance becomes the forefront motivation that results in both fashionable forward thinking statements and that of cultural appropriation or cultural appreciation. As performativity dances through our bodies, we can step foot in each costume we choose to put on – as a mask, both of warrior paint and of conforming made-up faces.

So what is to be Mexican…even race, is nothing but performativity – we are so mixed that this world will no longer be focused on the purity of a "mutts" blood… That is both beautifully inspiring and overwhelmingly daunting for me. Oh Mexico, Oh America, with so many identities – so much identity, how at times we become nameless… Both dead and alive, we are built of a cosmic race – with such mestizo, such universality – we become so universally limited.

Oh Mexico, we with so many races pump so many bloods while looking through the eyes of one animal. We hold the head of one with the body of another. For better, or for worse, we are made of many to become one… but just one?

Si, Mexico, they were right when they said

"Mexico, so far from heaven. Yet, so close to the United States"

"The Shard Table"
Draft #6

She,
He,
Therefore,
They.

We,
See –
& Therefore,
Be.

Them, There!

Us, Here…

You,
Gone
Sights set,
Set in suffocating stones
Still,
and stagnant

Stones, alone.

See – shhh – she, there!

Can't we,
Be…

Here?

& He,
she
Where?

65

Somewhere,
Nowhere.

For they,
They sleep upon safe,
Soft,
Shear silk…

For they,
Mask the makings

Making a mapped out majesty

Majestically,
& "Magically"

Yes,
They

Dine upon divinity

While, we –
We dine upon dimes.

Dance with discomfort
A fort of dis…

Diving deep into danger and dare

We dine,
Damned by disaster

We dine on dimes, with a dictated destiny

For she,
He,
Sighs upon another sight

Mounds,
Meaningfully- made
On their mountains

Leading
long-lived lives,

Leaving layers of unlawful,
Lasting,
Lies.

Casting crazed cries,
Into a crevice,
Of a crippled-cratered cancer

--

For we,
Fade away in fight

Forgetting fundamental falls,
Fighting for a future

For we,

Are simply on the other side of the table.

For fear of reaching out,
Fear of failing,
Falling,
Fucking fear,
Fear fucking,
Fuels the fantasy.

He,
She,
They,
There,

Us, Here…

But, *we*

Where?

"Compilations"

I feel I've found on Earth with you,
My baby,

You make me religious for your love.

Warm winds, catch the cool...

It's not as simple as a peace sign,

Soul Grange. Stretch marks,
Mark the land of my body.

Writing titles to poems yet written,
With the river that will never stop its flow.

"If you give her a taco,
She will return..."
The raining season,
It's never been oh so green.

Dried in a drought.

Brown-eyed girl,
I know you are tired,

Brown-eyed Girl,
I know you are drained,

Oh, my brown eyed little girl,

But don't you be ashamed.

Section Three: Writings of Love

"Speaking in Translations"

As I wake,
Floating out of my mind

Blissfully me,
Blissfully, how she can be

Play with me,
As free as a child,
Let us be what we use to be.

Hold me,
Into the waves of your sparkling shore

The further I am,
The softer the sand
The closer I am,
The rougher the land

Sparkling from afar, the lasting dream of a reality

Sparkling through her piano fingers,
As you transform her into a song

As I wake,
Dazing into your lullaby,
I become transfixed

…. & Translated

"LUMINOUS"
Lluvia de Milagros & Sarah Tepikian

Let me walk within your wilderness,
I want to sleep among your shadows.

I'm not lookin' for no sunny days,
I've learned to only trust showers...

So my flowers can grow...
And my tears shall turn right into snow

So let me walk within your wilderness,
I want to sleep among your shadows

I'm not looking for your withered gaze,
I've just learned to love the galaxies

So that my soul can grow,
This pain takes you with one blow.

And my tears shall turn into snow,
But only to become a winter-flaked glow.

So let me fill in your dark space,
And turn it into an everlasting grace

Let me walk within your wilderness,
I want to sleep among your shadows.

I'm not looking for no sunny days,
I've learned to only trust the showers...

Peace of mind within the sorrow
You're (or This) wilderness ...
brings me a new tomorrow

And here the dark turn into a rush hour,
When madness is my only power

Let my flowers break and grow...
And watch my tears turn into snow

So let me walk within your wilderness,
I want to sleep among your shadows

I'm not looking for no sunny days,
I've learned to only trust the showers...

For when I walk within your wilderness,
My love is shining

And luminous,

Oh, so Luminous...

"NEEDS TITLE."

Someone told me to
See this world anew

To birth and to bloom,

Yes, someone told me to

Feel this world right through

To see the lasting light
And believe this life is all
…Right.

To play with this worlds' sight
And embrace the beating of my hearts' right

Yes, someone told me to
Tie-tongue no-good rules

& Speak the language of a new-view

To love the very truth

But know it is all I once knew
That,
...The unknown
Of ones' youth

Yes, someone told me to

See this world anew

To birth and to bloom,

Yes, someone told me to
Feel this world right through

Then I found you
And to birth
And bloom

Is to breathe
This world in two

Yes, I found you…
So this world
Has become anew
And to live this life
On through
To birth beauty into bloom,

Is to dance this world
With you

Yes, Someone told me to
See this world a new
Yes, someone told me to

Feel this world right through

Yes, right on through
Feel this world right through
Right on through
…You

A letter: Intermission,
Spoken Rants to a Warrior

12:25am
West Oakland Bart Station
Heading towards Pittsburgh Bay Point

On Guard,
Aware, &
Secure-in',
Neva IN-secure.

These are the words in which I witnessed
the depth of my mans' eyes...

As I stared into his expression that turned into my Goosebumps, as
my skin rose and pulled the whiskers out of my tan brown skin – this
becomes the bittersweet reality of a clear Oakland land. Oakland
the land of the Oaks, anchored by a hidden gem, or should I say –
acorn. The very acorn that pulls us into one and centers us into
equilibrium... Waiting for the seasons to water, yet never "waits on",
for we are booming and blooming trunks in which we are grounded.
HIS expression, a novel that I read in more than a two minute stare,
the most everlasting wait for a train – Rather, an expression that told
a Lifetime of struggle and experience – An expression that spoke
without words – scaring off any fear, for we are the fearless. In this
moment as he aimed to explain to a wealthy man that of which we
are constantly guarded, I witnessed an expression of seventy years
to come...In which I hope to have the honor to see, for a lifetime.
That which I fell in love with – a protector, a lover, & most of all...

A warrior.

Dear Warrior,

To change apathetic attitudes is to change, mentality. To change mentally is to change culture… The frustrating part is, that to change culture is to engage mentality & therefore, spark attitudes. So you see, it becomes all interdependent with one another in a bittersweet cyclical nature of feedback loops. All man aches and heals in war; you just have to find the battle worth fighting for.

You are the artist, because you are the image that feeds the world around you, the director to your play – a play time prayin' and playin', same game, rollin' in one name.

Stay Revolutionary,
Rain Goddess,
Lluvia de Milagros

"Twin Flame[14]"

Twin Flame
We are the same

Flicker fully,
Our fire is purely

Incandescence
You become my essence

Spark from an ember
To warm my December

Twin Flame
We are the same

---

[14] Definition: A **Twin flame** is a spiritual (esoteric or New Age) concept describing a special soul connection between two souls. The twin flames are thought to be a template for an ancient/eternal type of relationship between lovers. [1] The fundamental thought behind this concept is that the dawning new era in human spiritual evolution will be a time when relationships foster enhanced spiritual growth between lovers, whereas in previous times and still early in the 21st century couples stayed together for purposes of physical survival and economical safety more than anything else. According to the mythology of twin flames, in the beginning of time we were created from one source,[2] that was split into smaller and smaller units down to two souls (and on rare occasions, halves of one soul) that would journey to Earth to learn and experience duality. They would reincarnate over lifetimes with this longing for each other.[3]

Burn like fire
We only get higher

Shared soul shall Neva expire
Our love will only inspire

Cut from the same chord

Your lips have me explored

Twin Flame
We are the same

Caught in syzygy
Twinkled brilliancy

You are my light
Piercing and bright

--

"Sun, she sang"

So why don't you take me by the hand,
And make love to the land,
(With me)

Every step we take,
Becomes our child

Deaf from the social noise,
I listen –
For the melodies of life,
Guiding naivety

In silence,
Melody sings the loudest

In silence,
She sings.

So take me,
Take me by the hand

Let the rustling of the leaves,
Become our breeze…

And enmesh with me,
As we lay stupidly
In the puddle of our mistakes
Let our youth be our purity
And let our errors be our God
Let the breath we exchange,
Be our air,

Be my winds that take
The flowers pollen,

To the very winds,
That stirs my
Mixed-Latin storms

Yes let our breath
Be our winds,

Let our sorrows
Roughen our skins,

So let's scare fear in one stare,
As we shed our insecurities

The way a snake,
Peels off yesterdays skin,
Rebirthing into anew

So take my hand,
But don't use it as yours,

Side by side,
Let us do…

What a chord does to a guitar,

What a mother does
To a child's cry,
What a brush does
To a canvass,
What spring does
To an April shower,
To bring its may flower…

Let us do,

What the touch of your lips'
Do to the windows of my soul

What the whiskers of your chin
Do to the fibers of my fingers

What the sun does
To my freckles
As what the blades of grass
Do to my feet
What the rhythm of a beat
Does to your ears,
As it rings.

Let us do,
What a child's smile
Does to a bitter man,
Such as the moon
Lights the night sky
What colors do
For the mind

Yes, let us do
What color does
To the blankness of dark and white

What a poem does to a lover's heart

As what a brother would do,
To a sister,
& Sister to a tribe

As mother would do
To a honey hive

As father would do,
As teacher would do
& Be an equal creator

Be an artist with me,
An animal – you & I

Let us do,
What time does
To every wrinkle
& Tell a story
Through the rings of our trunks,

A tree
Aging through time

With roots to hold this Earth down

Let us do,
What a muscle or bone
Does to the body
& Be my eternal strength

Be the reason I die
An old age,
With the heart
Of a 13 year old

And be the color to my melody

And be the beauty,
The same beauty
That guides a song,

The same gravitation
And internal equation
To guide the birds migration,

The same intrinsic fate
That guides a sad mans faith
The same beauty
That guides happiness
Throughout space

Therefore,
Do with me

What a mountain
Does from afar
Creating the land marks
For a flying bird

Afar,
Gazing down
Do with me,
As the mountains do
When a bird flies above
And ground me.

Take my hand,
And stay intentional.

As a father would with his son,
As he learns to ride a bike
For the very first time

As warrior would,
Defending in the wild

Wild, wild, wild heart of a forest,
The rush of a Russian River.

What a spirit can do,
In this beautiful life

Therefore,
Hold my hand,
& Be with me
The artist,
Of our own canvass

& Do what a sunset does
To the following morning silence

Be the cycle of a new beginning,
My dear sunlight,
Honey molasses,
Be my sweet Badu-sunrise

And sun-kiss my cheeks
With the rays of you,
You,
My sight,

My everlasting fight.

"Joining the Race"

Knock on wood,

But she won't open
Knock on wood again,

To become a believer…

She may not open,
But oh is she listening…
Through the cracks of the door,
As she becomes your believer

And she'll believe in you
And she'll be at your funeral

Because she'll swim with you,
When seas have dried

Nice, and good.
Yes, she's with you

Climbing the trunks
Of trees that have fallen

Nice, and good.
She's with you,

She's finally joining the race.

And she feels yet again,
Inspired and anew,
Creating her alias,

To join the race.

She sees the way you look out,
And she wants to wear those glasses.

So knock on wood,
Although she won't open entirely
She will unlock the door,
But only from the inside

Finally,
She feels good enough again

Not as unorthodox as she thinks,
Still- unique in nature,
Within every vessel.

And between you two,

Are the greases made
By the oils on your cheeks
Blushing,
As your lips relax sideways,
Cheeks
That has been pressing against a divider,
Of an old
Wooden door

Yes, she may be different
But so are you,

She may see in a different light
But it is you
That turned the switch on
And exposed the room
To rawness

"Just Passing Time"
Reflections & Rants

It is one insane journey that we muscle through in this double consciousness that provides the glasses in which we filter the world from. It is the constant process of learning to unlearn the very instilled systematic language that was spoken to our "history" and therefore stories. Nevertheless, once we recognize these moments of decolonization and embracing that which we are from and what we are about but what we still have the power to control as our future, then we blend the double consciousness into one beautiful fluid soul. I find it really interesting the themes that come out in words such as "Passing" and this internal battle we have that we are learning to unlearn. We are learning to forgive, but not forget. To accept AND reject, but not neglect... We are learning to listen, but not obey. We are learning the balance between our humanistic affection and our raging madness of sorrow. We are learning to fly empathetically, and at times, Apathetically. We are learning to feel free, FEARLESSLY. For we are in 2016, still learning to survive and not aimlessly drive. The concept of "Passing" is the process of identifying these moments of unlearning and double consciousness not as a "tragedy" but an ember that fuels a lasting light of fire.

Passing: "Grandmother India gifts a lotion to my sister called "Lovely" to wash away her tones of origin-ality."

Passing: "Grandmother Tia-Abuela-Hermana-Madremia says to the newborn mother, holding her little changita – she'll get 'lighter' as time passes, not to worry mija. An Hija turned Mija."

Passing: "Grandfather named her first born Blanca."

Passing: "Ok, I've asked you to please stop texting. I feel completely invisible. Dad doesn't understand me whatsoever, I try to reach out and believe me it's seldom and infrequent because I know he is so limited in his capacity. His response is always about how my well-being impacts everyone else around me, never can it be just about me. If I talk about divorce it's about whether or not HE can handle it. I feel like a prisoner… If I am having a meltdown its about public perception or how the kids will handle it. If I don't want to get out of bed, its about who's getting everyone ready for the day, ready for life. I'm here as a supporting actress.. I'm exhausted, I'm falling apart and no one notices except when I'm no longer there to serve their purpose but not because Im truly missed for MY purpose. And my therapist says I should take sleeping pills, but it does not take away my exhaustion, my exhaustion burns its own exhaust, thick and hardened smoke polluting my mind, giving me daily migraines."

Passing: "Tame your hair!"

Passing: "It's winter, I've got to go match my skin again and get a new foundation."

Passing: "Job Application: Position: Salary: Name: Joseph or José."

Passing: "Usually, I mix her bronzer with my Matte foundation so that I can get my mix up on the same color. But she uses 'nude lipstick' which is coffee on her mouth, but Chap Stick on mine. Medium beige and warm beige, always stuck between two shades."

Passing: "Ways to say 'Hello': Yo wassup, what's Gucci?: HAAAYYY gurl: Hola Mamita: Hey chica cheeks" Step into the office and through the classroom – "Good Morning, Good Afternoon, how are you? Hello. It is wonderful to see you, how are things?"

Passing: "She wears sugar-skulled painted faces to be artistic, with her friend who claims it is only the lighting and her Instagram black and white edit that makes her face dark – darkening and glistening 150 more likes than I."

Passing: "Tribal print bought in size two at Forever 21."

Passing: "He drinks in the name of Hip-hop and tells a sister to 'Get low baby, get low and touch that flo!' as he sings (Busta Rymes remixed 'EDM' version - #Twerkit") Forgets the reason why a beat strikes a chord in your soul, to why now it's cool to wear cornrows on a fashion catwalk stroll...

He drinks in the name of Hip-hop
As he dry-heaves and dryly believes
His dance moves are vulgar and naïve.

Drink to the name
As we tame the flame,
(Still, throw the middle to the game)
Cus' "fame" are the ones to blame.

He drinks to thrust,
On white mistrust
Painted and blinded lust
To what he thinks is just.

Passing: "We are going to Mission, SF today to shop... What should I wear? Let's go shopping for Mission outfits – I'm feelin chola-esque todayyy, ayeee."

Passing: "Cocoa butter vs. Shea butter vs. Olay vs. Merdma Stretch Mark removal cream."

Passing: "Mother babysits while her babies are at home."

Passing: "Wealth will always equal power. But power does not always translate into wealth. You can be poor and powerful, and you can too be powerfully poor, or full in poor-fully power."

Passing: "What are credentials? The study of other peoples opinions and perspectives of truth, solidifying them as your own – priding yourself and justifying your actions for the simple fact that you have studied the patterns of someone else's published works, someone else's reflections and outdated opinions. Passing in a space with no room left for originality and authenticity in your own perspective and opinion in time. Not as truth, but as personal thought – which becomes your only truth. Passing through someone else's truth, this is the power of 'credentials'."

Passing: Día de Los Muertos is not Halloween

Passing: Every ten year increment determines the era of a new law, the era of a new box to check off, the era of a new census – what box will you choose?"

Passing: "Oh, you know… I'm Just Passing Time."

The notes of young feminist: Inquiries

....

"Native American Women activists, except those who are "assimilated",
do not consider themselves feminists. Feminism, according to Jaimes, is
an imperial project that assumes the given of U.S. colonial strangehold
on indigenous nations. Thus, to support sovereignty Native women
activists reject feminist politics." **This is a quote that really stood out**
to me in the connection between <u>**true sovereignty and feminism**</u> **or**
political activism. *It is true, that to be successfully equal and politically*
just is to admit to a language of capitalism, regardless of whether one
agrees to or not, but accept it as a system that is in place in order
to work around it to change it. It is a never-ending cycle that begins
to replicate itself throughout all kinds of different communities and
ethnicities. This cycle of acceptance and rejecting in their process of
assimilating, nevertheless the indigenous women and feminist activists
disregard this completely. Assimilation, this double edged sword of truth
and inevitable ongoing western obstacle. Therefore, it is disturbing to
see that out of all reasons families break apart factor in with the issues
and themes around gender rights and identity. Thus, family dynamics
are formed as a result of shunning ones right and sense of identity. As
I continue to read into the Native American Feminism article, it was
surprising to me how the community does not define feminism because it
already is instilled in their indigenous culture this sense of equality and
respect. <u>***I recall seeing this same concept play out in my experience***</u>
<u>***studying politics in Mexico- the indigenous women in Cuernavaca,***</u>
<u>***Mexico as students prepared for yet another Mexican revolution. The***</u>
<u>***same revolution that my father went to visit in seeing what was being***</u>
<u>***done and if there were to be any success with student organizing,***</u>
<u>***reminds me of the ways in which even indigenous Native American***</u>
<u>***communities organize here in the united states. It is frightening to***</u>
<u>***see the parallels and similarities, Mexico's corruption to America's***</u>
<u>***illusions.***</u> *Another quote that stood out to me in this reading was the*
following, "We are American Indian women, in that order. We are
oppressed, first and foremost as American Indians, as peoples colonized
by the United States of America, not as women. As Indians, we can

95

never forget that, Our survival, the survival of every one of us- man, woman, and child, as Indians depends on it." Such a strong quote that **_illustrates this sense of exclusiveness as we have mentioned before in Black feminism, where there are constant misinterpretations and assumptions of the feminist attitude, when in reality the true womanist never prioritizes the spectrum of oppression. The indigenous women claim that it is not a gender issue but a civil rights issue pertaining a WHOLE that has been and constantly discriminated. Discrimination becomes evident not as a whole, it permeates society through its false identity that western culture decides to place on, when in reality it is the entirety of the mentality that as a whole, suffrage is constant._**

… ….

WORDS: It is a strange concept to me really in that there is such a fight at times and a struggle to make known, make permanent, and make law to the very words that we believe should classify who we are, or who we ought to be. When the day comes where we open our eyes to the reality of law and what it entails, from its liberating opportunities to the limiting framework of yet another series of words. To acknowledge something as radical even, or foreign, and alien to what one expects to what one interprets to what one can conclude from its truths. When you see, to acknowledge something as "radical" is to acknowledge ones ignorance on the matter. We mustn't connotate radicalism as something negative but rather as an indicator of where the natural human development faults and where the beautiful mind can enhance and grow. Similarly when one is a child, the child is egocentric and yet knows the social Norms of ethics and acceptable behavior. When the child is corrected, "corrected" and domesticated, guided elsewhere the child can hesitate – the child may resist, for the child wants what the child wants. This is not to say the behavior or concept in which you have introduced is wrong, but rather, the act is different and in a sense "radical" to naturally accommodate. Radical, in the sense that it is stepping out of the traditional normality of what the child is accustomed to. Radical, be the path less traveled by, or dare I say, less acknowledged for its mere existence. The very way that as a woman, I remain mysterious. "Mysterious", I resent such a word. I resent for when you make ME a mystery, you exotify me into who you THINK I am, trapping me into your fantasies and thoughts of what you want me to be, in the image reflected in you, your fairytale for what you think I am, not for who and what I am in the image of my own godessness. And what I am, is equal to you, and my fellow humanhood. See, it is not too different to the very way one exotifies this image of "sexuality" and all that it MUST or mustn't entail. The very way my own people, my own culture, breathe generations of pride and machismo. Too many times the blood of the warrior, the blood of the fiery fumes of fight confuses us for how we react to that of which seems radical. Chicano Men, (The power of myth and male cultural fantasy), myth holding truth in its philosophical form, realm, and arena – may it hold truth to an extent. Yet myth, by culture, by generation, and by the end of an old society as it embarks on the empire of anew, holds a truth, yes, but ONLY a temporary truth. I for one, learn by doing, not by memorizing. I learn by discussion, not by reading. I learn by moving, not by stagnancy. I learn by being, not by seeing. I am a participant, not an observer. And to participate is to be adaptive to the world in which evolves endlessly, magically, and beautifully every single moment of your existence. To progress with the tides of seas and the winds of the seasons. I am radical, I see, simply because I breathe a fiery worldly evolution of my womanly breathe, in which you fear from, envy from, and aim to study and put into your scientific understanding of how to categorize such a distinct power of the universe. I am universe. I am a Goddess of many galaxies that span a lifetime of generations, a lifetime of lovers, a lifetime of terror, a lifetime of me making tender and vigorous love to you and the waves in which this world breathes all day, every day, forever on. And let us "refocus" right back here into theory shall we, for theory be one of the foundations of higher understanding. Rejecting the binary is to accept that there is a binary in the first place. It is difficult in the process of unpacking and aiming to reconstruct, that the very process can take you in a whirlwind of ideas and concepts to a point of oblivion. Left for one to dance in their head. The binary, being the ways in which this world has now been split into two. bi·na·ry'bīˌnerē,-nərē/ adjective. relating to, composed of, or involving two things. "testing the so-called binary, or dual-chemical, weapons" Two sides creating a she-he, we-they, them-us mentality that shields us from finding the common grounds in coliving, is coexisting. In taking away the binary, one must understand the binary through different lenses in finding what is truly wrong of holding two sides. Can these two sides not at some point come together such as the yin-yan philosophy? It is that we take away completely binary, or is it that we redefine? See, even here, as I free write my thoughts I cannot help but feel already filtered by theory. Filtered and monitored. Here, on paper, does theory dance and thrive to the melodies of an academic solution. Yet the true accomplishment is to bring forth the integrity of theory into the revolution of praxis. In doing so, what do we truly accomplish? What is the aim of which we deconstruct these concepts if in praxis there is no true change? What is accomplished when efforts that spend long and endless nights tossing back and forth, eating up ones soul in deep analysis and reflection, torn by the tormented heart and the exhausted mind, what is being done by theorizing and trapping ones self in the names of the names of the names of the names of the names of the names of the names of the names and the names of the names of the names to the names of all the names in the names of what the names is the names. We run the risk in theorizing of creating more names than we can bear or can even conceptualize any more. The goal is to take away the binary, and therefore the goal is to see a better life, a change in what is seen as normality. A goal I can stand by, as we see clear discriminatory injustices in the world. Nevertheless, the binary, is to hold two, and life comes in two's. Nature, is in sync one, two. What does it mean to take away binary? What is the true accomplishment? And are we beginning to see in praxis. Stay Revolutionary. Revolutionary comes in two.

CYBORGS: "A manifesto for Cyborgs" by Donna Haraway – "We are excruciatingly conscious of what it means to have a historically constituted body. But with the loss of innocence in our origin, there is no expulsion from the Garden either. Our politics lose the indulgence of guilt with the naiveté of innocence." (199) Therefore, there becomes a very distinct predetermined definition and foundation for all politics and way of living for a cyborg. A cyborg, being a name that fills the void of fictional characters and "historical understanding" of the ironic denial of dominance – that which is what is called now as the "woman's experience". (The one who is not animal, barbaric, or woman). To have those three words in one sentence is evident to the evolving "progressive" or non-progressive development of woman. By studying and understanding in a secular light, in an extremist manner, and in one pair of glasses rather than a prism, one creates as Haraway has mentioned a "false consciousness" in which one replicates, models, or lives by the word of a theorized denial of that which is a false consciousness but is inevitably in the name of truth and epistemological understanding of a false reality – ironically, that of the reality in which a cyborg lives and is defined by. Fictional and yet true, therefore ironic in nature. "Epistemology is about knowing the difference" (203) The cyborg by definition is seen as a character that of sentinel being adapts mechanical abilities, which bring the mind to matter, bridges the inner space with the outer and as referenced in Haraway, it brings a bridge of a generation rather than a rebirth. Therefore, the concept being illustrated here is that the terminology fills a void – and in filling the void with this terminology, one naturally accepts the void as an existing entity. This reading makes me think of all the fictional characters portrayed in movies, the romantic and outdated images of that which is woman in our time – our time that still judges one on beauty, intelligence based on twenty second responses, and talents that contribute to the overall defined beauty (without intelligence). I could not help but think of beauty pageants and personal criticism on this image of the "goddess" and the national actress of perfection and womanhood. **"A manifesto for Cyborgs: Science, Technology, and Socialist Feminism in the 1980's"**

What is a cyborg? → "A cyborg is a cybernetic organism, a hybrid of machine and organism, a creature of social reality as well as a creature of fiction. Social reality is lived social relations, our most important political construction, a world-changing fiction. "(191) "This is a struggle over life and death, but the boundary between science fiction and social reality is an optical illusion." (191)

- *Lluvia de Milagros Carrasco – Professor Denise Witzig – Women's & Gender Studies – "A manifesto for Cyborgs" by Donna Haraway – "We are excruciatingly conscious of what it means to have a historically constituted body. But with the loss of innocence in our origin, there is no expulsion from the Garden either. Our politics lose the indulgence of guilt with the naiveté of innocence." (199) Therefore, there becomes a very distinct predetermined definition and foundation for all politics and way of living for a cyborg. A cyborg, being a name that fills the void of fictional characters and "historical understanding" of the ironic denial of dominance – that which is what is called now as the "woman's experience".*

REPEAT, REPEAT, & REPEAT is how we are trained to learn...

- *(The one who is not animal, barbaric, or woman). To have those three words in one sentence is evident to the evolving "progressive" or non-progressive development of woman. By studying and understanding in a secular light, in an extremist manner, and in one pair of glasses rather than a prism, one creates as Haraway has mentioned a "false consciousness" in which one replicates, models, or lives by the word of a theorized denial of that which is a false consciousness but is inevitably in the name of truth and epistemological understanding of a false reality – ironically, that of the reality in which a cyborg lives and is defined by.*

- *Fictional and yet true, therefore ironic in nature. "Epistemology is about knowing the difference" (203) The cyborg by definition is seen as a character that of sentinel being adapts mechanical abilities, which bring the mind to matter, bridges the inner space with the outer and as referenced in Haraway, it brings a bridge of a generation rather than a rebirth. Therefore, the concept being illustrated here is that the terminology fills a void – and in filling the void with this terminology, one naturally accepts the void as an existing entity.*

- *This reading makes me think of all the fictional characters portrayed in movies, the romantic and outdated images of that which is woman in our time – our time that still judges one on beauty, intelligence based on twenty second responses, and talents that contribute to the overall defined beauty (without intelligence). I could not help but think of beauty pageants and personal criticism on this image of the "goddess" and the national actress of perfection and womanhood. Yet they asked me to be apart of a pageant, here in the Bay, and the incentive – the chance to win a scholarship.*

Oh, yes, The Art of Repetition.
The Art of MANipulation.

… …

"Black women as a group have never been fools. We couldn't afford to be." (148) A powerful statement in the reading, "Introduction to Home Girls", that I really resonated with as a womanist myself, a feminist of color, in seeing the ways in which people find themselves justifying what exactly black feminism, feminism for that matter, but particularly black feminism really is. Similarly to how Barbara Smith had stated, that because people are either unaware or do not know the how to define Black feminism, many resort to reacting to black feminism or black social justice issues as a detached, exotic, and even outdated issue that is no longer pertinent to today's current day and generation. When in reality, it is having to refocus oneself not on this concept of "social justice" as a theory, a scientific analysis, or research database, it is to recognize how discrimination still exists today and where the womanist lies within it all. The "How", how social discrimination takes place, what social justice really looks like, and where are the red flags. Defining the "How" becomes a lot more complex than just stating obvious signs or even feeling as though because there may not be no longer racist signs that tell one when and where to use the restroom such as it was commonly seen in the 70's then in it becomes assumed that there no longer is obvious signs. The "How" illustrates the "What" and therefore forces one,

in the sake and name of survival, to adapt accordingly. Therefore, the "How" is not merely a passing time, an interest of study, or an intellectual topic to wine and dine over. The "How" is simply the tool in which to recognize, to inevitably accept, in order to adapt and move forward in any way possible. It is as if the womanist is in fact shifting gears, as if she were to be driving throughout life and here you see only a face, a made up body that takes this body of molecules from one to another. The very face and body that shifts gears, but never lets go of the wheel. The womanist, cannot afford to do anything else But. Contrary to common belief, it is in fact that "A black feminist perspective has no use for ranking oppressions but instead demonstrates the simultaneity of oppressions as they affect third world women's lives" (152) a statement that is so simple and obvious yet so profound in having to be reminded of those who simply do not wish to comprehend. It is quite easy to swallow the belief that all is settled in our current day, and we must then refocus our energy into a new field, and new industry, or a new movement. No, the woman must and will to survive, learn to shift gears.

Personal Reflections & Notes: Learn to play ball with the white boys and girls, learn to ignore the ignorant statements for the sake of not being the "smarty pants" who is constantly trying to correct those very small, intimate and social moments that be small but are incredibly significant. These moments of possible correction become instead moments of common acceptance and a natural state of complacency, which socially forces the womanist to become a bystander against her own will. Therefore, the "How" becomes as Smith stated, the very home truth that creates the revolution within and therefore, without throughout a lifetime of time and constant evolving change of nature, for we have already socially accepted so much that it has become an instilled nature at this point. Sadly. This then becomes an interesting link that I find with this concept of "identity" credentials. The journey that we all go through in trying to find a title to the already identity credentials that we are predetermined to have and carry along with us. These identity credentials that distinguish us as individuals but do not necessarily create complete separation unless we put power to those central differences in that very manner. The very criticism that I have that there is this almost competitive and even rushed process in claiming as many identities as possible for the sake of supporting something or claiming a side on a matter as if it becomes the only way in which one learns to navigate the world successfully. It is very similar to the ways, in which I use to observe the social dynamics and organizing tactics that were taken place in union efforts all throughout Oakland. The efforts are remarkable and humbling, all the hard work that goes into organizing the rights of service workers in recognizing the value of their worker rights regardless of what the workplace was. Nevertheless, the tactic most popularly seen was with employers is creating a cultural dynamic within the workforce that way that diversity was covered as a form of separatism and segregation as a best way to create a weak unit – and therefore an easier unit to control and maintain. I fear that this creates more than diversity, but rather diversity as a form of separatism and clashing amongst one another. Although, as Smith said that black feminist do not take the approach on prioritizing or 'ranking' oppressions, sometimes it is not that there is a ranking but rather a timing and sense of urgency that is pressing and worthwhile to fuel and give attention to. Sometimes what is needed in certain moments is the necessity for a autonomous institution. A institution that is run to revolt, and no not in a violent manner, but in nourishing that urgency and aiding to the most pressing needs. "It is absolutely crucial that we make our visions real in a permanent form so that we can be even more effective and reach many more people... We need more. I believe that everything is possible. But there are challenges we face as Black feminists that we can neither bury nor ignore." (155) This is the mentality most needed to not prioritize or rank but as Smith put it so eloquently, organize as a unit that can reach so many more so long as there becomes a solidified and strong unit that branches outward from a united starting point. Because if not, history will repeat itself and powerful stories like the "Fire" that takes you in a whirlwind of what it would be like if we could go back in time, will be the very ways in which our great great great grandchildren will look back at our time in history.

..

Lluvia de Milagros Carrasco – Professor Denise Witzig – Women's and Gender Studies – Inquiry – "This Bridge we call home" & "The Female Man" There is a lot of conversation that speaks on this theme of "self authenticity" and the personal narrative that is crucial in understanding abstract topics and ways of defining what gender and identity is. Understanding gender discomfort, lesbianism, and becoming separate to that which one no longer identifies is coming to terms with being able to piece together all that feels off in one's past, accepting it, and owning it "I'm not a woman! This voice isn't disembodied. It's a part of myself, barely articulate yet breaking out into awareness." There are clues all over in times that is easy to deny, reject, and detach from simply because it doesn't seem "right" and it seems all out of place – Maybe one is not "suppose" to be willful if they are not a man, maybe one is not "suppose" to like phallic things if they are not lesbian. Then it turns into this internal dialogue of what is personal inflicted doubt and confusion, to what is being externally influenced by that of Patriarchy. Intellectualizing all that is perceived and internally battled with, that doubt becomes the over-arching power, "Perhaps I wasn't really a lesbian after all." Or perhaps to identify as male is not to deny lesbianism but rather, separate that it is not lesbianism one identifies with but solely it is man – that doesn't make someone lesbian if they are born girl. The maleness is neither something to hide or deny, the maleness isn't the enemy – when many times we criticize and ponder on patriarchy feeling as though male, and maleness, is in fact the enemy and the construction of all that is created by Patriarchy. This is the very mentality that is dangerous to get stuck in, although personally, I think that the frustration and sometimes hatred that arises in becoming conscious is in fact necessary – but is by all minds, dangerous to stay in. To stay in it would require stagnancy and one to plateau which moves nothing forward and brings no change to the corrupted mentality that struggles with acceptance and empowerment in ownership of diverse identities. To ask and simplify someone's experience and sense of identity to one ethnocentric question such as: "How does it feel to now hold white male privilege" is ignorantly stating that there is an element of invalidation and over-generalizing those who all (should then) based on the logic of the question, face the same feeling – a feeling of male supremacy and privilege – when that just is not true for everyone. "Disappointment that this is the most urgent question that these women can come up with – a response dredged from an essential poverty of imagination. How can they reduce my amazing experience to this rote question?" For the question's logic is assuming that there is ownership in identifying with or embracing white male privilege. In this reading, many questions were brought up for me – what is privilege? What is it to be white? What is this notion of proving oneself? How do we prove ourselves without theatrically exaggerating and exploiting ourselves to simply prove our identities? And to WHO is it most important to prove oneself to? It reminds me of the reading "Female Man" where in part II, Jeannine Dadier had said "I don't believe it, balanced on one foot, (Nice girls don't do that), She climbed down the ladder with her books and put them on the reserve table. Mrs. Allison didn't like WPA girls. Jeannine saw the headlines again, on Mrs. Allison's newspaper. Woman appears from nowhere on Broadway, policeman vanishes." The two readings are interconnected in this topic and conversation of the body in its relation to the person (carrying the shell of a body), the ways in which society perceives and acknowledges standards for the body is based on our exposed forms of entertainment such as a Broadway play, the way we story-tell to the way we socially interact with those who chose a different path. When in reality, all are choosing different paths, "That is a real Earth Man" (The Female Man). It has been historically seen that, in Broadway women were not even allowed to play roles designed and illustrated for a woman, and yet those who acted out this role – man – was praised and honored when done a great job, of the role in which they were not meant to play. Now this is not to say that, man who claims a role of woman cannot be fully woman-ly, woman-like, or identify as woman – but it is worth acknowledging that there was a time where this was not even artistically open to that of the most artistic of them all – woman. "Sometimes you bend down to tie your shoe, and then you either tie your shoe or you don't; you either straighten up instantly or maybe you don't. Every choice begets at least two worlds of possibility, that is, one in which you do and one in which you don't – or very likely many more, one in which you do quickly, one in which you do slowly, one in which you don't, but hesitate, one in which you hesitate and frown, one in which you hesitate and sneeze, and so on." (The Female Man, VI) An interesting quote that to me sums up very beautifully these two readings in the points that I found were significant and stood out to me which were – the relationship that we have with our identity and that of our body is merely influenced by that which society sets for us to understand and identify with – anything outside of that can be trapped within intellectual justification and simplified questions that limit us still within a framework of a generalized understanding and definition of what identity should entail and look like in real life, when in reality we are made up already of so many different parts and hybrids of different experiences that despite changes, what stays constant is our personal truth and understanding of ourselves which can never be limited and defined by all around us that pours over us and overwhelms us in societal expectations, taboos, and understandings – lies and illusions in the bullshit beauty it covers in sugar covered colors, shit with sprinkles does not make the shit disappear.

……………………………………………………………………………………

Lluvia de Milagros Carrasco Inquiry – Professor Witzig – Women's and Gender Theory – Reading on Sandra Lee, "Foucault, Femininity, & The Modernization of Patriarchal Power"/ "A political anatomy" in which the workforce, the army, school, hospital, prison, and the manufactory becomes disciplines only to 'increase the utility of the body, to augment its forces – what was the being formed was a policy of coercions that act upon the boy, a calculated manipulation of its elements, its gestures, its behavior. The human body was entering a machinery of power that explores it, breaks it down and rearranges it." This concept that through institutions there becomes a subliminal and passive training that adds onto the educational, societal, and emotional development of an individual – in that, the institution detaches you such as the "dissociation process" that was referenced in Davis' reading, "The Making of Our Bodies, Ourselves: How Feminism Travels across Borders – (Colonialist Trope Or Critical Epistemology?)" It is the act of mentally convincing oneself that for the sake of one's education development or work, the body becomes a machine in which you simply

control for the sake of labor. In addition, the body becomes a "tamed"
and "controlled" shell of formalities and stillness. Conservativeness
now becomes a name for western structure and institutionalized culture
in which one may not learn, train, work, or live through free expression
but rather DEFINING the ways in which ones' body OUGHT to conform
rather than live freely. Therefore, our understanding and research is
guided into another realm of information, a realm that is nonexistent
based on a conservative definition of what is right and wrong for the
woman body to act, do, or express. It seeps now into research and
understanding of cultural development, societal ethics, and women
anatomy – again, it is resorted and limited to becoming the "political
anatomy" in which now conversations on a truly biological and what
ought to be scientific process becomes a personal ethical and inevitably
political debate. For the political is the personal in all that rises for
women's issues and ethical turmoil. "The body's time, in these regimes
of power, is as rigidly controlled as its space: the factory whistle and
the school bell mark a division of time into discrete and segmented units
that regulate the various activities of the day. The following timetable,
similar in spirit to the ordering of my grammar school classroom,
is suggested for French "ecoles mutuelles" of the early nineteenth
century – control this rigid and precise cannot be maintained without
a minute and relentless surveillance." (Davis) This becomes a model
that is parallel to that of a prison, and without being dramatic or
extreme, it is a training to "simmer" down and "behave" correctly –
Behave accordingly like a good little girl that you are. It inevitably
creates this shame and internal guilt that is then put on as a result of
anything that goes against such conformity. "Individualism" becomes
an extreme concept, a modern and contemporary "outlook" in life
where one is now forced to go against and tame the very nature of
a humanistic physical release. It is outrageous to say that only to sit
straight, never to slouch, only to be released to use the restroom and
only to be cradling a pistol must be the only right and correct formalities
of working, learning, and training. Therefore, as Foucalut's account in
(Discipline and Punish) elaborates on this very concept of the "docile
bodies" that holds a series of historical, academic, theoretical, and
still modern development of what results out of this systemic takeover

of the womanly body. This brings together this "dissociation process" which I referenced earlier as a physical parallel or connection in the same ways that (Kuhlmann) illustrates as the dissociation between feminist body theory and research or activism as it pertains to women's health. The same ways in which one can detach two topics although they are inevitably interconnected is only a way to create a safe space in which one can remain in this intellectual level and excuse oneself in creating any real difference. The bottom line is, if you abstract some topic when it is clearly related to one another than you create the very culture that western and capitalist authoritative powers do in creating segregated weak powers – it is all simply put, ways to weaken the intellect that could hold much more power and strength if they came together in unity and in foundation. An excerpt that was taken from Reclaiming Women's Bodies references the "Virtual Speculum in the New World Order (1999)" Haraway speaks on the the initial process that was established by white self-help involved women who critically looked at the medical establishment to simply look for remedies on minor medical issues that they were experiencing, which encouraged although informal and not organized institution, helped to encourage self-help and exploration of the body. Therefore the emphasis of OBSOS with women discovering their bodies or "recovering ownership of their sexuality and reproduction through knowledge of their bodies hat is the particular object of Haraway's critique – '...women ritually opened their bodies to their own literal view. The speculum had become the symbol of the displacement of the female midwife by the specialist male physician and gynecologist." (Haraway referenced in Davis' reading). This point that is crucial and extremely important in recognizing all these points that are interrelated and connected with one another by how the woman evolves throughout time and returns to these very intimate and private moments of exploration and knowledge that unfortunately becomes so detached that it can be lost at times – so lost that even middle class women come together, naturally organize themselves, and result in evidence and proof of the very detachment that occurs with what "ought" to be corrected and formalized, to the very taming of that very vagina. Taming that little ittle bitty vah-gin-ah, oh Gena the Gina – simmer down now?

Wags Standpoint - concept of "the second women turn cold" commonly known as "the bitch" the cold-hearted emotionless monster that gets things done. When does this happen? Through age? Through time? Through heartache? Through relationships? Through experiences? If we took a woman who's never seen society who's raised in the forest and threw her in the workforce, how would you prepare her? Had she never had heartache - had she never had work _ would she gain these skills to what we teach women? Is it cultural? Is it societal? Inspired by the first conversation confronting conflict that Karen and I had...

Angélica Salceda is a staff attorney at the ACLU of Northern California, where she focuses on economic justice, immigrants' rights, and civil rights and civil liberties enforcement in the Central Valley.

Prior to joining the ACLU as a staff attorney, Angélica was an Equal Justice Works Fellow sponsored by Fenwick & West. As an Equal Justice Works Fellow, Angélica led a project to identify and remove educational barriers impacting pregnant and parenting students in California's Central Valley. She authored a report titled, "Breaking Down Educational Barriers for California's Pregnant and Parenting Students." As a result of her report, the California Legislature passed and approved Assembly Bill 302 to ensure that lactating students in K-12 schools have access to a private, secure place to breastfeed or express milk during school hours.

Angélica is a graduate of UC Berkeley School of Law, where she participated in the International Human Rights Clinic on a project focused on the human right to water in California. As a student with the clinic, she co-authored a report titled, "The Human Right to Water Bill in California: An Implementation Framework for State Agencies."

While in law school, Angélica served as the UC Berkeley School of Law student body president, External Vice President of the UC Berkeley Graduate Assembly, and President of the University of California Student Association.

In those positions, she advocated for accessible, affordable, and quality education for students throughout the UC system. She also interned with the Center on Race, Poverty & the Environment, and worked on issues impacting disadvantaged unincorporated communities with CRLA's Community Equity Initiative project.

Before law school, Angélica was a 2007-2008 Jesse M. Unruh Assembly Fellow and was then hired as a legislative aid in the California Assembly. There, she worked on a number of policy issues, including environmental justice and immigrants' rights.

Of love and passing passions

Insecurities

I won't place my insecurities on you. I know they weigh you down like cumbersome golden coins in a sunken pirate's ship. Those insecurities are mine to keep in a secret vault nestled between my soul and heart. But they can creep up in the most inopportune of moments and asphyxiate your need for civility.

I'm unruly, I know—too unruly, even for you. In my inarticulate and shameless defense, it must be the feisty rebellious attitude that I inherited from *mi abuela*. An attitude that possesses all conquered nations and continues to suffocate even the weakest of us. The stubbornness has the same tainted history—one rooted in the need for survival amidst a wave of foreign conquest. I refuse to concede, despite imminent and unforgiving defeat.

But for the sake of your sanity, I will suppress it all.

My crude words are fiery flames that burn too painfully and ignite unprecedented word sieges without a means of escape. The white man labels these tactics irrational and unconventional—too savage even for the sympathizers. The crudeness runs through my prickly-pear-colored blood and flows through the ruins of my heart. When it overflows, the white man becomes collateral.

I am a Mexican firecracker of sorts. A righteous Sor Juana Inez de la Cruz. A fearless Maria Felix. An unceremonious Chavela Vargas. In your world, I am an unenlightened Mexican Jane Austen lacking sophistication and poise—too vulgar for your East Coast taste.

But for the sake of your sanity, I will suppress it all.

I shed tears of sorrow—often without reason. *Que chillona.* That is what years of colonization will do to a soul. I would know. But the Oscar-winning cry overwhelms you—it weighs you down. And yet, if I hold back tears, I am heartless, stoic, and without a hint of remorse. Oh the irony of conforming to suppressive standards!

My creative imagination creates unsettling scenarios from your silence. How crass of me. You insist that the silence merely means "busy." Too busy for my nonacademic, overdramatic, and burdensome talks. I impatiently wait for your perfect time to talk. It is usually sometime between the hours of "get over it" and "never."

But for the sake of your sanity, I will suppress it all.

You could spend your life smoothing away the rugged, uncolonized edges of my body until they protrude in your life no more. Then, I would be free of insecurities and social traumas. Just like you want me.

I tend to fall astray from meek and gentle ways. I complicate everything, especially for you. It must be my bureaucratic-public-education tendencies. After all, I am a product of public subsidies and I can never keep course on my own despite my efforts.

But for the sake of your sanity, I will suppress it all.

My Mexicaness ignites war and our fights are nothing more than battles of conquest. Unarmed against an army cloaked with entitlement, I charge while facing defeat. The result is bloodshed of tears for my tribe, and a cry of victory for yours—just like the history I abhor.

My rebellions never go unpunished and are quickly squashed. Spurts of protest are taken as military advances. It must be my savage *mestizo* nature—a nature that only an anthropologist can tame—causing all the turmoil. It must be all of those insecurities: the coarse hair that needs straightening, the English-Spanish switchback, the love for Mexican *corridos*, and the Popish loyalty of Latin America.

But for the sake of my sanity, I will own it all.

You call it, insecurity. I call it s*er Mexicana*.

--Sor Gitana

Una Mexicana on the verge of a nervous breakdown

The psycho-diagnosis reads: Mexican hysteria—a psychogenetic disorder that affects the feeble. Just like me. My name is on the list of newly diagnosed victims. It was bound to happen. The episodic rages and posttraumatic wailing are its corollary. It must have been your silent departure. That is what the psychotherapist says.

The slightest provocation will ignite it—like a silent landmine quietly waiting for its victim. The endless nights of sleep deprivation subdue me. You can see it in my sunken eyes and runny mascara that leaves black clumps of residue. I think it makes me endearing.

But really, it is just *una Mexicana* on the verge of a nervous breakdown.

The culture-bound syndrome has plagued all of my ancestors. It is their legacy to all born and unborn. It readily involves an outpouring of emotions for a lost love, a rush of caffeinated nerves, blackened nights of unguided wondering, and bounded seclusions with callous memories— all easing the nail-pulling pain of abandonment.

The prescribed remedy is a pharmaceutical-cocktail of sorts: spiked gazpacho sloshed back with Prozac. It tends to muzzle the rapid-fire insults in my native tongue that you know all too well—those that drove you away. A hit of nicotine eases the craze and I float into the unknown. I convince myself that I'm just auditioning for a part in one of Almodovar's melodramas.

But really, it is just *una Mexicana* on the verge of a nervous breakdown.

When the hysteria kicks in, it ruptures through my soul creating a complex narrative of abandonment and a desire for revenge in the tire-slashing kind of way. Reverting back to those days of swigging tequila for breakfast, I sink into the cold cotton sheets of an empty bed embraced only by the ghosts of the past. I stare endlessly into the ceiling as the hysteria evolves and begins to possess every inch of nerve.

There is no hint of remorse—not when possessed by hysteria. Nothing really matters. Not even you. And yet, I hide like a coward behind a numbing dose of tequila and nicotine. I stare hopeless at the receding cigarette burning silently and see my life recede with it. Only black ashes remain. It must be a reminder that I am dust and unto dust I shall return.

But really, it is just *una Mexicana* on the verge of a nervous breakdown.

The madness leaves me tongue-tied and under a thick San Francisco-like fog. Secluded to the empty terrain of regret that you left behind, I stand under the Bay drizzle and allow my tears to blend with the mist while the screeching breaks of a trolley muffle the sobbing. The hysteria is unforgiving like that.

The virgin bottle of sleeping pills next to my bed keeps me company—it is the only unconditional love I have left. The nail-biting nerves want it that way. Alone and distressed like an unwanted mistress—that is my unforgiving destiny. That has never been a secret despite my hallucinations. My madness adds one more to the collective Mexican hysteria of forsaken women.

And really, I am just *una Mexicana mas* on the verge of a nervous breakdown.

--Sor Gitana

Corazón de Obsidiana

They say her heart is carved out from Mexican obsidian—sharp as a butcher's blade.
It can pierce through skin and bone.
Man or boy.
It can cut you.
Just ask those few.
The volcanic glass is fierce.
Merciless they say.

They say her fine obsidian has no emotional brittle edges.
It's true—none.
Each edge has been finely smoothed with time and tears.
Weeks and years.
Chiseled away by stone-blade heartaches.
Of the scorching kind.
Polished with swabs of rejection.
In a tumbler stew.
Free of cracks and fissures they say.

They say a volcano spewed out her heart in liquid form—an eruption that devoured the earth.
Causing plight like Mount Vesuvius under a cloud of fire.
With a hint of satire.
The rivers of felsic blood slithered through the earth.
Creating crevices.
Deep with grief.

They say the volcanic glass reveals her most sacred pains.
Traumas dressed in lustrous colors.
Of the ancient kind.
Those that conquered her by forcing her on her hands and knees.
You can see it all.
Through the mirror of the blackened glass.

They say her obsidian heart has killed a few.
It has sliced through lies like a surgical tool.
The big and bold.
New and old.
Slaughtered those that ransacked her sacred village.
Skinned those that consumed her gold with gulps of greed.
She killed them all with the edges of her arrowhead.

They say there are no obsidian flakes left behind that belong to her heart.
No volcanic ash that spewed that day.

Some have dared to search.
Just for one.
But none.

They say her heart has been hidden within the womb of the earth.
Stripped from a glass case where it was observed in the British museum.
Far from the pains of the endless stares.
A perfect artifact now resting within the walls of her mother.

They say her heart is carved out from Mexican obsidian.
Of the pre-Columbian kind.
Not the tainted one.

--Sor Gitana

Departing Melody

She sat at the edge of an abused flower-print mattress staring incessantly at her chipped, maroon toenail polish. The confusion flickered like an iridescent light with a faulty electrical circuit. She bit her lip to hold back the wailing. A drop of blood trickled down her splintered lip as she replayed his words over and over like an overstressed polyvinyl nearing its end.

"I cannot do this anymore," he said.

That was it. The two-second song violently echoed throughout her ghostly mint-colored bedroom, pouncing on her eardrums. With every unsavory gasp of air she took, the song trembled louder muffling the recognizable apathy in his voice. The song contained no explanation for the hasty departure. It was simply an unmelodic symphony marking the culmination of a farce but joyous journey.

As she sat there, the psychedelic lyrics condemned her to a permanent state of distortion and sporadic trances. The shamanic powers of the deafening song vibrated throughout the tremulous walls of her life. Hallucinations ensued, evoking abstractions of love with color spectrums of her pathetic life.

With every screech of solitude that she released, the feedback of the modal melody kept on growing louder and more sinister, just like the palpitations of her heart. The quiver of her restless lips joined in choir as the throbbing tunes journeyed through a labyrinth of vindictive pain. In protest, her body withered.

Her cries never ceased—the departing melody kept them alive as her acid teardrops crawled through her eyes and ripped through the flower-print mattress.

Defeated, she whispered, "I cannot do this anymore."

--Sor Gitana

The Weight of Happiness

The scale reads differently every day.

It started at 125—the weight of happiness. The night you called, I checked. I stripped down in front of the mirror smudged in your fingerprints, unpeeling every layer of clothing that reeked of your essence. First the sheer blouse you hated—too revealing, you claimed. Then the legendary softly-pleated, black skirt that swirls with every San Francisco breeze. My fingers struggled to unclasp the hook until the skirt finally melted off of me. There I stood, naked. Dressed in tears. Staring at the scale.

My right foot stepped on the digital scale as the left one instinctively followed. It started at 125—that is what it read.

The anguish of the rejection stifled the hunger. That is when I stopped eating. Nothing for days, except for my Mexican remedy—a few swigs of Oaxacan mescal to induce the sleep and subdue the sorrow. My stomach grumbled in protest as the *aguardiente* slashed-and-burned the pain. That is how we play the game—we Mexicans. Tranquilizing the feral beast with shots of fiery liquid.

The posthumous body transformation was quick. My malnourished face wilted into my cheekbones. Not even layers of heavy make-up could conceal the sunken eye sockets that grew with every grumble. The morning contractions of hunger immobilized me. Kept me in bed. Skinny. Skinner. Like you would have wanted.

My body was weak—unsustainably weak. The nicotine binges did not help. They just masked the hunger with clouds of smoke. The voices told me to eat. Eat something. Anything. Just eat. But books were the only thing I devoured during those days of famine. They nourished me. One after another I wolfed them down with tears.

When the scale read 117, I called you. Just one last time to confirm the death. I could hear you breathe rejection through your silence. It was surely dead—rotting in a coffin, six-feet under. I set the phone facing down on the nightstand and reached for my notebook to write a few words: *the mystery begins today.* With a few tears, I mourned the death and then drifted into dreams.

This morning I stepped into the shower, allowing my toes to feel the shivering cold tiles. I needed to cleanse what last remained of those useless memories—to forget you. I stood under the showerhead, tilting my head back to feel the pins of the water drop on my face. The water rushed through the waves of my hair and onto my toes. After a few minutes, I shut the water and stood in silence listening to the grumblings of the soul.

I stood in front of that mirror again, naked and dripping in water. My feet rested at the edge of the scale, ready to mount my reality. My right foot stepped on the digital scale as the left one instinctively followed. It ended at 122—that is what it read.

I must be reaching happiness again.

—**Sor Gitana**

The Petition

Her nails dug deep into the coffee stained mattress that once echoed their sounds of love. Like an unforsaken child grasping her chest to avoid the heart from tumbling, she pleaded with the universe,

with Pachamama,
with Tonantzin
with any God or Goddess that would listen to her unsettling petitions.

With every hollow cry that emanated from the blistering pain, her body wilted into the crevices of her arms like a discarded Calla Lilly to subdue her mental turmoil--the crude reality of a love tossed into a mortar drenched in solitude and crushed into pieces by the torturing pestle of his words.

She tilted her entire body back and sank into the waves of the mattress, while suffocating the sobbing shrieks with a crisp pillow over her face. The muffled petition demanding his return reared its thorny head through the loose threads as her feet submissively

dangled

down

the edge

of the mattress.

Her empty soul swam against the currents of the bed sheets that were drenched in his scent. For a second, she thought she heard his heart beat emanating from the aching muscles of the mattress but it was only the wails of the overstressed bedsprings.

He had been gone for days.
Weeks, maybe.
Perhaps he was never really there.

And yet, she could still hear the sounds his body made when they made love on that coffee stained mattress.

--Sor Gitana

I was …

I was the human subject of your social experiment--
the one selected from a menagerie of wild beasts.

You were gentle and deferential as you cornered me into your cage.
You caressed me and blessed me to assure me it would all be okay.

I was the wildest and most untamed--
the one with the aboriginal mane and foreign name.

You inspected my lips and hips and measured my tits.
You pulled my hair and spanked me bare to tame my fits.

I was the crudest and rudest of them all--
the one that devoured her young.

You abhorred my savage nature and forced me to belong.
You conditioned me to only sing your song.

I was the one that fit your fetish mold--
the one so ethnic that you could call your whore

You ransacked my inner voice with blistering fire.
You paraded me in front of the masses like your aboriginal child.

I was the Malinche that guided you through your conquest--
the one that translated your broken gringo Spanish.

You created a legacy of psychological pains.
You tortured a culture and slashed my savage veins.

I was the wildest and most untamed...
Now, I stand in silence and afraid.

--Sor Gitana

83 Proof

We sipped the words of the great masters.

Bolaño.
Saramargo.
Galeano.

In a martini glass.
In a hipster unmarked bar.

--Sor Gitana

Adios

Her favorite word is "goodbye."
Adios.
She says it softly.
Kindly.
Lets the emotion dwindle into a whisper.
Until all that remains is a calloused whimper.
She serves her "goodbyes" with a shot of indifference,
Without a *quizás.*
Her smile swaddles the words.
Bitterly.
Like desert salt embracing the rim.
Her "hello"—a citrusy preamble.
A welcoming "goodbye."
She dreams of "goodbyes."
…how she'll tell him.
That rattling tone of the blast.
Sin ninguna esperanza.
Floating through the ruins of memories.
Wilting into her lips.
Apathetically.
She is addicted to the rush of "goodbyes."
A craving for her corner buy.
In all forms of liquid, rock, or smoke.
La droga del corazón.
Each ounce of despair—her high.
One thorny dose at a time.
Her "hello" is a dormant ambush,
Tactically dressed in underbrush.
Preying for the weak.
Silently.
…sipping the gust of dawn.
She sings the melody of "goodbye"
A war song that tremors.
Each letter chiseled in the air.

Adios, adios, adios.
It plays on "repeat."
…just one more time.
Her favorite word is "goodbye."
Un *adios.*
Un simple adios.

--Sor Gitana

She returned the words …

On a crisp cold winter morning she said goodbye. She repeated the words someone else had used against her—threw each one back into the universe. It was her turn to say goodbye this time. On her own terms. With her own words.

She was gracious enough to repeat them with a smile. Then a departing wink to seal the deal.

She said it all but not before making him feel wanted.
Cared for.
Loved.

The night before the ambush she warmed his white skin with the heat of her brown rage. Kissed his forehead as he slept. Gently. Admiring his loveless lips until the sun awakened. Slipping her tender legs between his like eager roots underneath a tree.

When the clock struck 3 o'clock, she offered him water, only to clear her own throat. Then, a kiss, never telling him it would be the last. A biblical betrayal.

She even left a razor on the bathroom counter for his morning shave. Turned up the heat to ease the cold that penetrated through his feet.

At the sound of his alarm, she slipped out of bed to prepare his last breakfast meal. He did not anticipate the savage ambush that lurked on the horizon. She followed their morning ritual--silence poured over a bowl of mediocrity. Always smiling even if she had to force the emotion through a straightjacket of indifference.

He must have thought she was opening up emotionally. Embracing the infamous spirit of vulnerability. Accepting of the ambiguity that came with the once-a-week visit. Deferential to the timing of the colonizer's watch. Giving into his power trip because they all do …

But during that morning drive as she drove him to his stop, she knew the words were coming because they were stuck in her throat ready to ambush him. He leaned in for a kiss on the cheek, like a missionary kissing a third-world child. But his lips never fully kissed her. Perhaps he feared contracting her leprosy and open sores of poverty.

"See you next week *querida*?" he asked.
"No," I responded.
His look of acceptance only made the remaining word easier to expel, "Let's just be friends."

--Sor Gitana

The Unhinged Truth

The night before the yearly celebration to *Oxtoteotl*, she slept with the colonizer. She entered his one-bedroom apartment with her regalia draped over her arm. He welcomed her with the gaze of the white man eager to exploit her identity. She greeted him with a kiss as a welcoming gift. It was all she had. There were no gold gifts this time.

He reached out for her *guerrera* dress and hung the embroidered art piece on the bedroom door. The weight of cultural exploitation hung with it, almost unhinging the wooden door. He paused for one minute to admire each stitch, each deity, and each silk ribbon that adorned the dress. It sparked a voyeuristic thirst that could only be quenched with his savior complex.

He reverted back his colonial instincts and shoved the Malinche to the edge of his bed. He peeled away each layer of her clothing until she became Eve. Ripped off pearl buttons and burst through her seams. Then, he gently shoved her onto the edge of his bed and suffocated her with cultural greed until they both drifted into sleep.

That morning she left. Left a note that read, "This warrior is off to battle." She pulled her regalia off the wooden door and marched towards war...

Once at the battleground, she covered her hair in a fan of feathers. Bright red ones that stood above her. Like fingers attempting to touch the sky. She danced his silence away with spins and jumps, and swam with the smoke of the copal as her bare feet cracked. With every slight move, she took it all back. Reclaimed her culture and unhinged the door of oppression while the gringo just slept.

The day of the celebration to *Oxtoteotl*, she wept. Her battle wounds caused by silence while she suffocated underneath the weight of passion.

--**Sor**

That's what he wants ...

Nestled underneath the crisp aroma of spring,
in a smoke-filled Las Vegas hotel room,
a half-empty bottle of scotch signaled acts of libations.

She lay there in bed with him, embracing the silence,
staring squarely into the gaze of the ceiling,
ushering in the spirits of solitude with each sip.

He released the agony of his heartbreak with a sigh,
and she did the same,
but not before she cleared the silence from her throat,
to tell him about the other.

"I decided to reveal all of my imperfections to him--ragged edges and all. Even my strong taste for Mexican *corridos*. I blast them from my stereo when he's in the car," she proudly proclaimed, referring to the *gringo*.

His chest perked up as he prepared to slash through the veil of silence.

"That's exactly what gets him off!" Don't you see it? Don't do that. Stop feeding the untamed fetish," he proffered while stroking her hair in bed.

"But that's what I like to do. I can't help my urge to turn up the *paisa* music. By the way, did I tell you what his name means in Nahuatl?" she said.

"Fuck, don't tell me. He appropriates names too? That is what they all do. They have ripped away everything from us and now our names too?"

She admired his rage against the *gringo* but wasn't quite ready to cede.

"He's nice, though. He even brought me gifts from his vacation trip. Two rocks--little tiny ones from a beach somewhere that I will likely never visit. He brought them back in first class!" she shared somewhat jokingly.

The irritable eye roll washed over his face.

"Wait, he also brought me back one bar of soap and exotic dates that he later ate without sharing," she said.

"Don't give into his whiteness. Can't you see that you'll just spend the rest of your life making excuses for his exploitative cultural urges?"

She scoffed at the idea while leaning toward him to rest her head on his shoulder.

"But what if he really likes me?" she insisted.

"Listen, he just wants to culturally appropriate you--extract your cultural value for his own street cred."

She sipped what last remained of the diluted scotch and smiled at the irony of being in bed with him but talking about the *gringo*.

"Do you think he just uses me to practice his Spanish? Is that all I am to him? Free practice?" she asked him.

He slipped down into the covers and closed his eyes. Her body followed as her question simply lingered.

She curled up next to him and slept it all off.

--Sor Gitana

"Calm the fuck down"

Five drinks in, he reeked of eagerness and desire for touch.
I warned him. Just this once. That's all I could commit to.
His Brooklyn swag couldn't handle it.

He rolled up the sleeves on his denim shirt,
The one he handed me hours earlier,
for me to iron. I did.
Creased and starched.
Vato-loco style.

He leaned in to swim across the river of disinterest,
to deliver an unsolicited kiss and whisper,
"I like you."
I winced.
Clinched my lips.

I warned him. Just this once.
That's all I could commit to.

"Stop playing hard to get," he said.
And hauled me towards him,
gripping my sanity.

"Don't get attached," I rebuked,
arching an eyebrow and retouching my lips.

I know his type.
Easily attached.
Man-of-the-house kind.
Needy as fuck.
Good for a night.
Two, if I have time.

"Calm the fuck down," he shouted.
'Cause I was the crazy one.
"You ain't straight in the head" kind of gal.
Too H-two-H for him.
Hard to handle, he claimed.

But I had warned him.
Just this once.

So why can't he calm the fuck down?

--Sor Gitana

One drink and weekends

We had one drink.
One evening.
Because a friend insisted.
I resisted.
I just wasn't in the "falling in love" mood.
Or the fucking mood.
Not this month.

Fine. Just one drink.
That I can do.
But I'll pay.
I wouldn't want you getting the wrong idea.

I played with my phone that evening.
Chewed through the color of my straw.
And sipped the bourbon in gulps.
A sign of disinterest.

"I can only be friends,"
But he thought I was playing games.
Once again, hard to get.

Then I broke it to him,
Mentioned my move away from the Bay.
I even moved up the date,
from September to May.

"We can still do weekends," he said.
"And make weekends official?"
All that despite knowing me for two seconds.

"After we hit it off,
we will have a weekend relationship,
until you move back to Oakland.
Into my big ass house."

I swear, he said that.
Verbatim.
Because he had a plan.
But I rolled my eyes.

Fuck, I even paid for drinks.
And this is how he pays me back?

No more, "just one drink."
But tell me, how do I get my money back?

--Sor Gitana

Loving in Spanglish

Dias como Today

There are days when I wake up with an obsessive need to write.
The anxiety boils like an *hoya de frijoles* with the steam ready to pop
the lid in a burst of raging fury.
The sensation leaves me paralyzed,
como muerta,
in bed as I contemplate the morning light that pierces through my
window.

Así fue el día de hoy.
The desire to write was asphyxiating
como el humo de un fogón en pleno invierno.
It took possession of me,
forcing my hand to clasp a pen firmly between my fingers
until *palabras* appeared on paper.
Y como sucede desde que te conocí,
I wrote about you.
I drew your eyes with ancient words
in Spanish and *Inglés*
porque mi corazón así te conoce.
I wrote *desde el fondo de la cuevita de mi alma*
in a language only you and I know
a secret dialect that is etched in hidden stones.

The writing left me desiring you.
Me dejo queriéndote this morning that all I wanted for breakfast was
to sip on *el café de tus ojos*
while savoring *el pan dulce de tus labios.*
I wanted to feel the sugary grains of your laughter on my lips
while the honey dew of your touch rejuvenated my skin.

Y yo seguía en cama como tamalito envuelta en mis sábanas
remembering *como dormías aquellas noches*
when all I could hear was your beating heart.

Y para que lo sepas
I watch you sleep each night.
I witness how your body caves into the mattress
while you place one arm under the warmth of the pillow.
Hasta sonreís when you sleep.
Y con pincel I try to capture it all
in a time capsule

of words

that I can read back each time I wish
para recordarte.

Pero no es igual like having you here
a mi lado

But I like you free too.

Me gusta verte volar solo into foreign lands in search of life.
You are meant to fly *como águila*
y me satisfecha con solo verte bailar through all the skies.

The sweetness of your flight falls onto Earth caressing the wind, lightly.
Y eso es suficiente para mi.

--Sor Gitana

Yo Chiflo

I whistle to the beat *de tu alma*
como un pajarito en pleno vuelo.

I whistle in the shower
al hacer el desayuno
and *cada segundo* I get.

I wonder if you can hear it
through the wind *en esas tierras lejanas.*

I whistle your name
with each syllable dancing off my lips
como chapulines.

Sonrió when I whistle.
I even whistle *cuando sueño.*

When I stand waiting for the elevator
chiflo al verlo bajar cada piso like a leaf from a tree.

Chiflo during traffic jams
while I travel through the artery of El Valle Central
dead stops, stop and go, go and stop.

Y cuando escribo, I also whistle
al final de cada sentence
or mid-sentence
dependiendo en el tempo.

Chifló al sonido de tus ojos.
Con calma and profoundness.

And while I walk down the streets of Fresno
or San Pancho

o por donde quiera que este,
también chiflo to see if you can hear me
or see me.

I whistle *porque* you inspire me to sing your song *de viento.*
La escuchas?

--Sor Gitana

Jupiter and Venus

Pensé en ti tonight
as I stared into the sky's abyss
to witness the rare dance
between Jupiter and Venus.

Los dos planetas stood
as if suspended only by love
staring into each other's cosmic past
con una sonrisa pintada
con los rayos del sol.

All you had to do was aim your eyes towards *el oeste*
around sunset
and there they were
mirándose el uno al otro
captivados por los misterios del infinito universo.

It was a beautiful dance
amidst the darkness of the summer sky
an endless dance.

One that had certainly taken place before
and now it was being repeated before our eyes.

Si solo pudieras haber estado con migo
para observar esos cuidadosos pasos de los planetas,
creo que te hubiera encantado.

We could have spread a blanket over a river of grass
and settled our bodies above the cotton fibers
to observe the majestic duet.

But instead, we observe tonight the same design,
through different eyes, and different sides.

Tu desde el sur y yo desde el norte,
observando el mismo sistema con un mismo corazón.

And although the dance will only last a night in the sky, it will never
die in my eyes.

--Sor Gitana

Safe Travels

You make my *corazón* smile--deep and wide.
With each beat, it expands through the walls *de mi pecho.*
I was content before you stumbled into my life.
Era increíblemente feliz because I thought I had it all.
Y llegaste tú con tu sonrisa de Dios to make me smile.
Y me di cuenta que me faltabas tu.

Te quiero, te quiero mucho aunque quizás no siempre lo sientas.
I live in a world that thrives on vagueness yet demands clarity.
From politics to law, your value depends on how well you hide your cards.
And I've learned to bluff to survive in that male-dominated world.
Porque si no, te comen viva.

There's been no room for vulnerability *en esta vida*
because tears don't win a case, they lose it.

En mi profesión, cada mañana me tengo que ajustar my emotional straight jacket
to suppress it all.
Triste, lo se.
Pero prefiero sobrevivir and be effective in igniting the flame of justice,
and professional stoicism is the game to play.

But I want to be vulnerable with you.
Me quiero dejar querer.
Te quiero querer.
I want to lean *mi cabeza sobre tu hombro y decirte que te quiero mil veces.*
I want to prioritize you--your happiness.
Quiero estar ahí cada ves que me necesites.

But the fear (of what, I'm not sure) leaves me paralyzed sometimes.
I'm scared of things even when there's no need.
Tengo miedo of getting caught watching you sleep in the morning,

of pressing my ear against your chest to hear your heartbeat,
and even of kissing you sometimes.

My mind has a way of holding back the flood of emotions that are trying
to burst through my soul.

I admire many things about you.
But perhaps what I admire most is your ability to be vulnerable,
your ability to genuinely love without restraint.

That is a beautiful gift.

Y me comprometo a luchar día con día para ser un poquito más así.
Me comprometo a aprender de ti.

Te extrañare mi sol. Extrañare tu calor y tus besos mi Júpiter.
Regresa pronto.

--Sor Gitana

At home

I feel at home with you.
I hear your voice echo
with the crisp sounds
of my white bed sheets
as my body drifts through the linens.

I can see your eyes
through the flickering light of the candle
as it sits on the armoire, patiently,
with the flame rising with each breath.

I can feel your warm body touch mine
with the hot gust of the Central Valley air
that empties the room.

I can taste your lips
with each sip of my lemon-ginger tea,
warm and gentle
percolating through my taste buds
like honey bees.
I can see your shadow roaming my walls,
dancing tenderly with the light,
growing bigger with delight.
…you're always home with me.

--Sor Gitana

Un Nuevo Lenguaje

I've learned a new language, thanks to him.
O quizas I picked up a new pen.
That could be it too.
Because *cuando escribo*, it sounds so different.
Como musica and I know it's him.
Porque antes era dolor, aunque no fuera mío.
It was my inner Chavela or Cherrie,
O cualquiera de esas chingonas.
And now I'm still them
Pero festejando amor.
Dejandome amar, like Sonja said.
Y yo amando.
Because bodies were made for loving.
For caring.
Y así lo quiero querer a el tambien.

--Sor Gitana

At home

I feel at home with you.
I hear your voice echo
with the crisp sounds
of my white bed sheets
as my body drifts through the linens.

I can see your eyes
through the flickering light of the candle
as it sits on the armoire, patiently,
with the flame rising with each breath.

I can feel your warm body touch mine
with the hot gust of the Central Valley air
that empties the room.

I can taste your lips
with each sip of my lemon-ginger tea,
warm and gentle
percolating through my taste buds
like honey bees.
I can see your shadow roaming my walls,
dancing tenderly with the light,
growing bigger with delight.
…you're always home with me.

--Sor Gitana

Un Nuevo Lenguaje

I've learned a new language, thanks to him.
O quizas I picked up a new pen.
That could be it too.
Because *cuando escribo*, it sounds so different.
Como musica and I know it's him.
Porque antes era dolor, aunque no fuera mío.
It was my inner Chavela or Cherrie,
O cualquiera de esas chingonas.
And now I'm still them
Pero festejando amor.
Dejandome amar, like Sonja said.
Y yo amando.
Because bodies were made for loving.
For caring.
Y así lo quiero querer a el tambien.

--*Sor Gitana*

Tuesday Nights

Did you know I dance?
Tuesday nights.
Aztec-warrior-like.
With copal.
The dance erupts.
Like thunder in the night,
as the beat of the drums rejoice.

Did you know I cry?
Tuesday nights with wine?
After the battle is done,
and before the dawn comes down.

I think of him,
his chiseled face and grace
the tears burst through and
I forget about you.

Did you know I write?
Tuesday nights?
Poems and prose,
none worthy of more.
Each word is hate
on occasion just one page.
love and compassion is rare
because I write about my affairs

Did you know I love?
Tuesday nights with just one?
Although I rotate them all.
To vary it some.

--Sor Gitana

Sus Regalos

He gifted me a new voice,
one more suited to me,
a Spanglish varnish,
with switchbacks,
como yo hablo.
He gifted me a pen,
with an ink of love
and an inkwell of laughs,
para escribir mas,
during those solemn nights.
He gifted me a song,
que viaja por el viento
like a leaf under the desert sun,
que llega a mi mejilla
and sits there like a freckle.
he gifted me a good-bye
on a Friday night,
"I don't want to waste your time," *me dijo*
so I squeezed out a smile
to respond, "It's been fun."

--Sor Gitana

Enojitos

His anger peeked through his smile,
right through the gap
between his two front teeth,
when I asked him,
"seguro que no quieres comer,"
for a second time.,
he gave me a look of *"déjame en paz."*
las misma cara de cuando I had to work nights,
he'd go silent for days,
autonomía, pensé yo
pero creo que eran berrinches
for a little more attention.

--Sor Gitana

Apache Tears

The *abuela* left her a medicine bag,
before the last gasp of air.
"Cuando llores, put your Apache tears in there *mijita,*
Y prende una vela so that no one will know."
Because in our *familia no se llora.*
You sweep the dirt right under,
quick and sly,
like when an unexpected guest arrives,
"Correle porque ya llego julanito."

The first time I cried for him,
I reached for it.
Before the sniffle tickled,
or the tear trickled.
Porque yo soy Hernandez.
And no *hombre* can see me cry.

In there the tear went,
nicely pressed,
into its satin bed,

I painted a smile,
wearing tall and proud,
the *abuela's* embroidered *huipil,*
to feel her energy,
su abrazo,
that cries,
"there's no hollering creek here, *mijita."*

His silence echoed,
even howled,
like a struggling soul in purgatory,
rechinando como uñas sobre un pizarron,
as he peeled away the serenity.

The lump in my throat swelled,
como un globo,
on the verge of bursting,
right through my *pecho,*
like a spear on hunting grounds.

He called me his *cariñito,*
su corazoncito,
even gifted me a *rebozito,*
acompañado por un librito,
"to make up for the silence," he said.

Mi abuela warned me of all that:
the power struggle,
the constant tug-of-war,
of loving full-throttle.

"That's not real love, *corazon.*"
Not when there's power.

When he said,
"I don't want to waste your time,"
I saw the mountains cut through the sky,
to force the downpour of the night.

His words,
forced me off the cliff,
dropping into a field,
of bleached bones,
and despair.

"Pero no llores," I remembered.
Because my tears just turn into stone
and there's been enough of that.

He must have known,
that crying is my most precious secret,
each Apache tear a war song,
that only my medicine bag knows.

"...and when the right one comes along,
you hand him each obsidian stone you hold,
and if he hands you his,
you know your home."

--Sor Gitana

Geography of Love

Bourbon Tears

She sat near candle light,
on Derby Street,
gently,
devotedly,
sipping the tireless minutes away
of the implacable rat-race,
her gaze aimed
toward the crushing weight
of the quivering stars,
contemplating destiny.

The honey liquor waited,
patiently,
for her hand to grasp its fate.
A ritual of many nights--
of bourbon fights.

She dressed in solitude,
drenched in the sweet scent of happiness,
ruminating ancient memories,
While the winter California storm,
turned into New York's spring.

And so she sat,
pondering about her destiny,
pressing her ear to the wind,
to listen to its cries,
it told her to go home,
to her desert throne.

She swam,
perhaps just a minute,

against the suffocating waves,
of memory …

…the pebbled soil where she played,
of endless rows of orchards …

Destiny had branded her at birth--
to be a picker of sorts,

with a green plastic bucket,
and assortment of nicely starched bandanas,
for the scorching heat.

…sorting through the swarm of almonds,
picking between two fingers,
only the most beautiful,
the flawless caramel ones,
never letting those hands stop …

Like her mother,
just as fierce,
just as happy.

But the wind blew,
sweeping her feather-like future,
far from the scorching heats,
of California's fruit basket,
far from the invisible,
concentrated poverty.

And so she sat,
sip'n,
on the rocks,
restraining the urges to go back,
because no one ever does,
because there is no American Dream there,

no prestige,
just pounding defeat,
with back-breaking pain,
and shots of cortisone to produce gain.

"... you won't find happiness there,
only broken dreams ..." he said.

I ceded to the honey liquor,
its color resembling the pollinating bees,
those that dove through almond flowers,
in the middle of the summer heat.

I took one sip that led to more,
until my eyes burst,
and bourbon tears poured.
And so I cried,

for my desert sun,
and parched lands,
because no one gives a damn,
when its rural land.

-Sor Gitana

Northbound 99

Last night I traveled through the main artery of the Central Valley just as I have for many years—accompanied only by my thoughts and music blasting from the stereo. I know every turn and pothole with great precision. My foot presses on the break at the sight of every highway patrol patiently hiding near dark orchards or down a dirt road. They've never caught me—not yet.

It's a beautiful journey despite the loneliness, especially at night. Yes, especially then, when the stars peer through the dark veil of the sky, some brighter than others. They guide the way up Northbound 99, through my childhood memories. They follow me, never losing sight of me but often fading with the overcrowding of the neon signs.

Yesterday, I cried. The reservoir of sadness broke. It always breaks during that northbound drive. The slabs of concrete aren't enough to confine the waters sometimes. As I move farther and farther away from the roots that anchor my childhood, I feel lost and uncertain about my journey despite the glaring signs that signal San Francisco.

Somewhere between Merced and Modesto I feel my heart tugging. The patch of darkness between those two points invokes thoughts that spark questions and an unsettling urge to turn back. I turn up the stereo with the Spanish *corridos* to muffle the thoughts. Nostalgia then takes over. The fear multiplies exponentially. My only consolation is the thought of seeing you at the end of my Northbound 99 journey. But not today. You won't be there.

Driving up Northbound 99, I leave a trail of tears to retract my steps someday. I leave all the sadness on that journey. All the fears of urbanism. All the fears of not belonging. They stay there. On the black asphalt of Northbound 99.

I can feel the transformation of myself with every mile I travel. I can see the signs for the 120 West, to San Francisco. All the Chevy trucks evade the exit, but I take it. All the Range Rovers and Priuses take it too. The 40 mile-per-hour turn onto the 120 West curves into another world. The Spanish *corridos* turn into radio static. I leave the cosmic background noise on for a few minutes and then begin to hit the scan button. There's nothing. And then, the Sunday Slow Jams come on. I'm in the Bay. No more *corridos* about my grandfather's time. Just slow jams, smooth R&B, and a sea of commercial lights shining as I enter Livermore.

I hit some hills and think about our drive in Marin—the New Year's Day drive. The sadness begins to evaporate or maybe I'm just driving faster than they can fly. Either way, the first smile that emerges is because of you—my love for you, found in the Bay Area.

Olvera Strolls

My heart smiled with every step we took down the cobbled Olvera Street. It was a magical journey—one that I would only take with you. And as we walked through every doorway, we entered into a world of colors and art that we shared together. The bright red and orange flowers blossomed permanently inside those brick walls. The ceramic figures stood quietly, watching us as we strolled through the rows that showcased Mexico's past. Their ceramic hearts smiled too as they witness our happiness.

We zigzagged through the crowd of visitors, always holding hands. Sometimes we pushed through the crowd and I held onto you even tighter. Stepping over stones longed traveled, we witnessed Olvera come alive. Its music sung melodies from every corner. Its people laughed uncontrollably. Anyone stepping into the world where cornhusk flowers bloomed and paper mâché dolls thrived was certain to be struck by happiness. Just like us.

There was so much to see. There were beads, jewelry, Veracruz-inspired linen clothing, and *huaraches* of all shapes and sizes. There was even a beautiful hand-tooled leather purse to admire. It was as close as I would get to showing you my beautiful Mexico.

The smells of the taco stands whisked away our hunger and the taste of the *agua fresca* quenched our thirst. The sweetness of Mexico was displayed behind glass counters in the form of *dulce de guayaba, tamarindo, cocadas,* and other treats dressed in sugar. It was a sweetness fit for the bellies.

The storefronts were decorated in hand stitched dresses and a sea of *huipiles*—one for every occasion in life. Sprinkled throughout the shops like morning dew were also not-so-subtle reminders our of dead dressed in *Catrinas.*

And there we were, observing a world dressed in colors while holding hands, strolling through the cobbled Olvera Street, possessed by happiness.

--Sor Gitana

Amber Butts is an educator, writer and artist living in the Bay Area. She is a caretaker and behavioral therapist for foster children with disabilities. She enjoys multicultural, alternative educational settings and facilitating workshops with youth on identity, healthy relationships, community building and self-love. Amber's works at Saint Mary's College of California has instilled a lifelong passion for creating responsive systems that welcome faculty, students and staff with non-normative lived experiences and instead provide practical tools to work against oppressive structures (without alienation, shame and fear). She believes that consistent communication and positive interdepartmental/ inter-office relations are important to the overall health and maintenance of every institution. In her spare time she enjoys storytelling and reading comic books.

Brown Girl

Promise me

That you'll never forget

loving yourself is holy.

That you are worth

More than what they

Show you.

Mother Tongue

Bandage

Smother

The not like me

But almost like her

Smell.

The opening up

of old wounds

That change the air.

She wasn't allowed to breathe

In the language

She's known all her life.

This is how we all die.

Success

must not only mean me

It must mean my entire family

I do not carry them

We carry each other

This revolution must mean

That they touch it

That they understand

That their struggle is named

In this

That we all matter

The women.

Nana

Bubbie

Mama

You

Me

The World.

Baptism by Air

We are children of the sea.

Protected, loved, blessed

With an abundance the eyes can not fathom.

My existence is not dependent on how desirable you find me.

I will be here regardless.

This freshness.

How To Listen

Do people count on you for support?

How do you show up?

There is an art to how your ears move

When you listen.

Seeking Help

Promise me you will find help

Each time you find yourself

Falling back into oppressive histories

Every time you try to find the white poison

Underneath your skin

Promise me that you will make it

No child should

Know what it's like to have a grown man

Punch them in the eye

The too sweet, wet blackness

That always comes after

You remember betrayal.

The brokenness

The realization that

He planted his feet just right

That it wasn't reflex.

That he meant this.

This splitting between the thighs.

The eyes.
Everywhere.

We were taught to

Clip the clouds

Pull the moon closer

And never complain.

Especially in destruction.

Today

A Black girl was thrown

Across a classroom

The world says she deserves it

She only wants to feel sand

Between her toes

They will not call her a child

How dare she be child?

Brave, outspoken, forthright.

Yesterday

A Black boy was burned

By pistol.

The smoke promised reprieve

His mother asked for it

And what she got was

An interrogation into his history

A justification for his death.

They will not say murder

It is accident

Bound to happen

Misfire of the gun

Pictures of him doing "bad" things
Are everywhere

It makes the evil

That took his life "good"

When I have my child

I will tell her

This world will never allow you to be

Young

And you will always be guilty.

I am so sorry

for creating you.

Rebirth by Fire

Who better than us

To show what it looks like

To rise from the ashes

To be salt

Air.

Created after dust flies away

Soil remembers your name

And you are always seeking water.

Small

I pulled a tooth

Out of my skin

Yesterday

It looked exactly like the uncle I lost

How can this be anything

but truth?

Absolution

The girl

Sea

Skinny sandals cracked like skin

Brown stories

Swimming into the water

And forgetting what it feels like to float.

Stop seeking absolution.

Stop trying to find salvation for the bad choices.

We are already the saved.

Articulate

Whenever I hear, "You're incredibly articulate"

I hear, "Damn, they taught you well/ If only your skin were white/

How can you belong to those animals?"

Every time this happens

I remember Caliban

And I weep.

Body

Where are the sex educators who look like me?

How will I get to know this body?

How will I be able to talk about how I hurt?

Euphemisms for colonialism

Body.
Black.
Black body.
Brown Black.
Slave.
Slave.
Seductress.
Whore.
Undead.
Superstitious.
Backward.
Coward.
Dog.
Animal.
Almost-man.

Reality Check

How many more Black folks have

To die before we call it genocide?

We will call it bone

Lilt of foot

Black on Black violence

But never what it is.

The Turn From Feminist to Womanist

Leaving a space that was never really there.

And missing it anyway

Aching for it

For it's ghost heart and ghost tears.

Declining to let it hold you again

Because you never really mattered.

They used you.

On Trying To Breathe While Listening to Mansplaining

If I received a dime

Every time a white boy came up to me

Trying to explain the pitfalls of minority groups

Like I am not here

Like he is not disrespecting my blood

As if he doesn't know that I am

And we will always be smarter than he.

Black Girl, Why Are You Here?

I am here because of my nana.

The late night walks into hell

For us.

You taught me that there

Is triumph in refusing to run.

On Spankings

"Black children need to be spanked."

Growing up my grandmother would spank us with a switch (a branch you get off of a tree) or a cowhide or something else she could find. As a child, the lines were clearly drawn out, "here is what you can do" and "here is what you can't", "here's what's accessible to you because _____" (there was always an implicit reason, but the underlining one was because I am Black. When I saw white children roaming freely, I remember feeling anger, jealousy and like I was cheated.

I didn't understand. And as I talk to my multi-ethnic friends who have children (or don't) I still have things that jump out for me. Like when I'm in Trader Joe's and I see white children throwing temper tantrums, pulling things off of the shelves, pushing baskets into others a part of me is angry, but this anger is not directed at the child. It's at the parents whom I feel like don't think about how their children/ parenting styles can negatively effect/ add stressors to the way the workers do their jobs. Insert a different setting; a library, restaurant, or a farmer's market. These things happen and I believe they tend to reflect something about class and culture, about entitlement and convenience, about ideas, movement and freedom.

I also believe that Black folks experience a heavy load of cultural mistrust on a daily basis that causes them to be at least cautious and at most fearful, in these situations about how they/ their kids should "behave" in public. I remember attending a conference and meeting Joy Degruy, author of Post Traumatic Slave Syndrome and her relating these instances of anger, discomfort and caution to the treatment of slaves. When a slave master said "My, that boy right there is _____ " a mother would have to counteract that with "No, this boy is lazy, shiftless, etc" in order to not threaten/ encourage him working in the fields/ being seen as a threat or authorizing him to go to another plantation. There are many layers to this destructive behavior of breaking the spirit.

On Sexual Harassment in the Black Body

The first time I was catcalled, I was 10 years old. Two grown men were in the store telling me I'd be a knockout (language here, notice how when we talk about girls and young women violent language is always present) when I got to high school and that the boys would go crazy over me. One of them looked me up and down so much that I dropped my hot Cheetos and ran out of the store. I remember feeling like I'd done something to warrant the attention and inappropriate behavior. I now know that I hadn't.

I remember that feeling being amplified in High School when older men would park at the corner of our school and honk at the young girls walking. I remember feeling like someone stole something deep within me when I'd see some of my classmates get in those cars. I remember classmates and their mothers (directly or indirectly) telling each other that catcalling is a compliment and/ or cute, that we should be thankful. One of the most frequent comments went something like, "Men can't help but lose their minds over you" (mind you, we're 13-14) and that we should take it in stride.

So now we're expected to take responsibility for the male's actions because we are pretty/ attractive/ children/ have something that they like/ smiled/ were polite, etc. while they continue to be creepy, disrespectful and outright scary. As young girls we are told dual narratives: that we own our bodies and should not let anyone touch it and (the other) that we should look pretty, invite attention and take it as a compliment when men treat us as objects/ things to be owned, that if we are uncomfortable, something is wrong with us because everyone likes it.

As an adult, I see the same thing. I see women giving out real or made up numbers because of fear, pressure and/ or because they feel like they don't have a choice. We encourage these ideas when we tell other women that there's no big deal or that these behaviors are expected. The worse part about these messages are that they are presented as if they've always been that way and that they won't change. When catcalled I try to really have a conversation about street harassment, try to relate the behaviors to that the person doing the calling is displaying to something else so that they may get an idea of what they're doing, find alternative conversations that we can have, etc. I do carry a knife at all times, just in case. I also get frustrated as hell at myself for being the one that is trying to relate, to point out issues and offer alternatives, but I feel it's better than not doing anything.

Classes on harassment and respect should be mandatory in Elementary School. That's where it all starts.

If you're interested in someone, be creative. Do NOT be a creep. Talk to your women friends about their experiences with this topic and change the way you do things. (Don't use the things they say as tips to continue the behavior deep down but appear less creepy. Be genuine).

And women, please stop co-signing sexual harassment. Do not tell women they are being harassed because they're "pretty" and that it's okay. It is NOT okay. Women have internalized patriarchy and misogyny to the extent that they reinforce it through their interactions with other women.

We all gotta do better.

Myrna Santiago was born on the US side of the border, but grew up in Tijuana, Mexico. Her family migrated to Los Angeles when she was 12 years old. She learned English at Robert Louis Stevenson Junior High in Boyle Heights, then received a scholarship from the "A Better Chance" Program to attend prep school in the East Coast. She went to Phillips Academy, Andover and from there to Princeton University, where she graduated with honors and a degree in Latin American Studies. Upon graduation in 1982, she went to Mexico City for the first time on a Fulbright Scholarship to study Mexican immigration to the United States. Shortly thereafter, she moved to Nicaragua to witness the Sandinista Revolution. She worked for a human rights organization there for four years, then returned to the U.S. and pursued graduate work. She received her PhD in History from the University of California at Berkeley. Having taught at Berkeley and Mills as a lecturer, she joined the Saint Mary's College history faculty in 1999, where she teaches Latin American history. She is currently the Chair of the History Department and sits on the Advisory Board of the Women's and Gender Studies Program. She also has a very conflictive relationship with Che Guevara.

April 9, 2014

Dear colleagues, friends, and family:

In case you are wondering, I a wearing the traditional dress of a Triqui woman, among the most marginalized indigenous people of Mexico. It was made by the angry and loving hands of a woman.

Thank you all for your presence tonight and to my colleagues for honoring me. My deepest gratitude to the History Department for welcoming me with warmth and kindness fifteen years ago; and to Women's and Gender Studies for recruiting me into the program that long ago too. Both of you have created a fertile intellectual environment for me and a true sense of camaraderie. I have learned a cartload about teaching from you and I have grown and thrived as a scholar because of you. Despite my anger, I know Saint Mary's College is the place where I belong.

I teach because I am angry.

I am angry because at every turn, I see the corporatization of the University, not creeping toward us, but racing to swallow us whole. The drop in state support for scholarships for students; the increase in public and private disparaging of the liberal arts - in particular –and the university, in general, as useless in an economy that prefers cogs rather than thinking human beings; the adoption of the gospel of efficiency as the preferred handbook for administration; the demands that we measure what we produce like so many widgets in an assembly line; the heightened reliance on lecturers and adjuncts and part-time staff—the whole package that leads us down the road to becoming Sweatshop U, stripping us of the single most precious treasure we have at the university, which is academic freedom; the freedom to think critically, to think against the norm, to express ourselves out loud and discuss without fear. The University is under attack by the same social forces that have led the country and the world to a level of concentration of wealth and inequality unprecedented in history, with all the suffering that means for people every day.

I am angry because we here in bucolic Moraga are not immune to the structural violence such a system represents.

I am angry because one of my Chicana students spent so much of one semester shuttling home to negotiate with authorities who deported her brother to Mexico. His parents brought him to the US when he was a toddler; Spanish and Mexico are not native to him. My student became a translator, a lawyer, an advocate, an intermediary, a one-woman support system for her family as she helped them navigate the hostile and byzantine maze of the federal immigration bureaucracy –to no avail. You can imagine how that ordeal affected her emotionally and what it did to her performance in the classroom that semester, not to mention the chronic sadness now settled over the whole family like heavy, cold fog that will not burn off at all.

I am angry because another of my Latina students received frantic phone calls from home for weeks as her mother and younger siblings faced eviction from their apartment. She was the one who sought alternatives to the threats of violence coming from the landlord. She was the one who her terrified younger brother called from jail, caught as he was by those death-eaters that hover above so many poor communities in the Bay Area and beyond, the drug economy that is always hiring and incarcerating (and killing). She was the only one in her family who was employed, because her mother had been hurt on the job, left without the necessary means to support the little ones in the house. The stress took a toll on this young woman's health. Her brilliance was not reflected in her grades either.

Both of these two women hold down jobs, are active in social justice work on and off campus, and carry a load of student debt much too heavy for their slender shoulders. In addition, too little financial aid, they both merit prizes for their intelligence, their work ethic, their dedication to family and school, and their perseverance in the face of tremendous adversity. But of course neither fulfills the qualifications we as a community have established for recognition because such rewards tend to favor students whose families don't have to confront injustice on a daily basis.

It's been over ten years and I am still angry because of the literal violence that took Catalina Torres from us. She should have been here tonight. She is in spirit as we remember her. Cata was angry. So angry, in fact, that when she was a student here she joined a whole lot of other angry young women and went on hunger strike in the shadow of De La Salle. Their demands were simple and radical: that the College takes seriously the rape of women on campus. Those students were responsible for the creation of the Women's Resource Center. And thanks to them, the WRC today is a model for other schools to follow in its dedication to inclusion and equality for all students, no matter what their sexual identities, race, class, or ethnicity may be. Yet as I read that a woman is hurt by a man in her life every few seconds in the United States, and practically every semester on our campus too, I am angry that I clearly have not done enough to teach young men not to rape women. I am angry that we collectively have failed to teach generations of men to renounce violence.

I am angry because part of the legacy of globalized exploitation is the gigantic mess we are leaving to our youth: a planet gripped by a fever that demands that we as teachers prepare our youth to unleash their anger and their imaginations (and their love) to make the planet whole and livable for their own children.

I teach because I love.

Who can remember Cata's smile and not love her? And not smile at the memory?
My love is not a paternalistic love that believes I know better than young folk because I have been around the block once or twice. My love is not maternalistic, wanting to surround energetic youths with bubble wrap so they won't scrape their knees when they stumble and fall.
My love is complicit.

When I hear, "Mom, my rock band is going on the road this summer all the way to New York and back," my love responds: whatever you need, day or night, just call me (and it also wishes: take me with you!).

My love is liberating.

It opens windows in the classroom, letting in wind, rain, snow, dust, sunshine, herbicides, noise—discomfort, lots of intellectual discomfort but in a very safe and loving space where both students and teacher can time travel to places and times past and explore with reckless abandon and passion that cannot measured.

My love is subversive.

It pushes students simply to read and think, until their eyelids droop, their eyelashes fall off, and their brains hurt: to be critical, to question the world as it has been given to them, and to consider that another world is possible.

My love is conspiratorial.

For when students do become critical, they realize that institutions, including Saint Mary's College, talk the talk but often don't walk the walk. Then they look at me with incredulous eyes and sometimes they say, "We are so mad! We are going to put a tent city on the lawn, and we don't care what the president says!"

My love promises: I will have your back. Because if I taught you well, if I loved you well, you should be angry.

My love is solidarity.

No matter how unrealistic the dream, how utopian or seemingly crazy the idea, how overstretched the wings, how colossal the mistake, how painful the fall, how broken the heart of idealistic youths, my love tells you: I am with you. I will scrape you off the pavement and help you limp along until you can walk on your own again.

My love is absolutely celebratory:

I celebrate Alex and Nicole, both professors of history at big universities now, lecturing in Latin America and African-American history, respectively, to hundreds of students at a time. Both are angry.

I celebrate Andres, an English major, with a minor in Women's and Gender Studies and a dollop of Latin American history courses under his belt, who made it his mission while he was a student at Saint Mary's to redefine and refashion for himself and his peers a new Latino masculinity and leadership style. Andres is returning to California to teach in San Jose schools next fall, after a long stint teaching Latino children in Arizona. He gets really angry sometimes.

I celebrate Brenda, the first student in 150 years of Saint Mary's College to major in Ethnic Studies. She designed the major herself, unfazed by the fact that she would be a major of one, without a cohort or peers, because Brenda is brave, and tough, and with a mind sharp as a razor blade.

I celebrate Karen, the first student in 150 years of Saint Mary's College to spend one semester abroad in Colombia, all by herself, without a program behind her, because Karen is fearless, and courageous, and smart as a whip. I haven't asked them, but I am pretty sure that Brenda and Karen are both angry.

That's why Brenda and Karen, who entered to learn, like Alex and Nicole and Andres, will leave to lead; to lead us all toward a more just society, like the Saint Mary's graduates working at the Monument Crisis Center are doing: Elizabeth, Josemar, Armando, and the interns Rosa and Alexander. In case you don't know, the Monument Crisis Center in Walnut Creek provides nutritious food and multiple services to families in crisis, and it is totally staffed by Saint Mary's grads, both men and women who became critical thinkers in our classrooms and took seriously the Lasallian mission to be in solidarity with the poor and work against injustice.

They lead us by example. So let's show them something: if there are any angry women in the audience tonight, please come up and join me.

Together, angry, and not, I want to ask you, my peers, to make the commitment to making sure that Saint Mary's truly is a college that changes lives, that it lives up to its mission of inclusion and equality, that deliberately practices the art of non-conformity in all its possible manifestations, and that intentionally sees teaching and learning as a subversive praxis.

And all of it because, in the words of that flawed and extraordinary human being, Che Guevara, we are "motivated by profound feelings of love."

Thank you.

May love continue to write its own chronicle,

To be continued

...

About the Author

Lluvia de Milagros was born in the Bay Area where she spent most of her time growing up, traveling to every nook, city, town, cafe, museum, and bookstore that Northern California could offer. At an early age, Lluvia could be found any given day journaling, reading Calvin and Hobbes, "collaging" her bedroom walls with music posters and CD covers, playing and sadly destroying her grandmothers' wardrobe (pre-thrifting era), dancing, singing, always taking her talent show group performances too seriously, listening to her grandmothers' old Mexican folk tales and ranch songs, cooking potions and new creations that were never edible, painting outside to paste real flowers and leaves to her canvasses, and making up her own games with family and friends. Growing up always creative and imaginative, she became acutely observant having spent so much time with her at the time, single working mother. Lluvia was a single child living in a mixed generational home of aunts, cousins, her mother and grandparents, where she learned to speak Spanish as her first language and early on became exposed to a community of strong, hard-working, independent and fierce womyn. After having experienced a kidnapping and rape in her early years in High School, Lluvia returned from a Treatment program in Utah to graduate on time at Notre Dame High School in downtown San Jose. Once completing High School, she went off to change numerous majors - Psychology, Sociology, Environmental Studies, Teachers for Tomorrow Program - to finally arrive to Women's and Gender Studies. During her time at Saint Mary's College of California, she completed her minor studies, one summer in Cuernavaca, Mexico then returned to continue teaching throughout the Bay Area in different service programs. Over four years, Lluvia performed numerous shows with her spoken word pieces, was asked to publish on different media forums and has been interviewed by different radio stations on her creative pieces and poetry work. Lluvia involved herself in numerous student and non-profit organizations in and out of University, was apart of the union efforts her freshman year to unionize Saint Mary's in over 50 years. In addition, joined a Chicana Feminist Writers Collective that was based out of Berkeley and later that year helped coordinate the schools' first Hip-Hop club named "Elements". By graduation, as a full-time student and now published author, Lluvia is set to pursue her ambitions in the arts – music, creative writing/screenwriting, scholastics, and politics through what she believes to be an artistic and accessible public platform. Throughout her life, she has witnessed discrimination and trauma for being an ambitious, intrinsic, talented, charismatic, and young woman of color, which has only inspired her even more to resist and challenge the standard of beauty, intelligence, legitimacy, creativity, originality, and power. In all of her publications and creative performances or artistic pieces she has expressed her passion in multiculturalism, transnationalism, queer studies, ethnic studies, youth empowerment, environmental ethics, education equity, civil rights, and diverse inclusivity. Being the daughter of two elected officials, Lluvia has always believed that she is independent yet parallel to her and her parents' work. However, she resists the idea that she is successful through and under the iconic images of her parents. Lluvia de Milagros, believes overall in the power of the womyn author who has been too many times historically erased -

"I am a sister, I am a partner, a scholar, a thinker, an observer, an outgoing introvert, a daughter born in April, a granddaughter holding the heart of a warm house of Abuelitos, Tías, primos, and crispy lightly burnt tortillas always on the comal. I am a dancer – only when the summer season brings its blanket of warmth and sun-kissed memories that have yet to be made..."

Printed in the United States
By Bookmasters